WALT WHITMAN
ON LONG ISLAND

*A hitherto unpublished engraving of Walt Whitman
by George Rupert Avery*

BERTHA H. FUNNELL

WALT WHITMAN
on
LONG ISLAND

Ira J. Friedman Division
KENNIKAT PRESS
Port Washington, New York/London

EMPIRE STATE HISTORICAL PUBLICATION SERIES
Number 91

Library of Congress Catalog Card Number 78-134275
ISBN 0-8046-8091-6

Manufactured in the United States of America

Published by
IRA J. FRIEDMAN DIVISION
KENNIKAT PRESS
Port Washington, N.Y./London

*This book is dedicated to my mother, Jean Rogers
Funnell, who infected me with her love of history
and her respect for the sturdy men and women who
settled Long Island.*

Acknowledgments

The Author wishes to express her thanks to these persons whose particular contributions along the way made the preparation of this material a pleasurable and rewarding venture: C. H. MacLachlan, former Editor of the *Long Islander,* for his valuable suggestions; Mr. and Mrs. Walt Whitman Swertfager for their generous cooperation in making the Whitman Family Bible available for photographing; Mrs. Alexander White for exhibiting her private collection of photographs and records that document the history of Whitman's Woodbury schoolhouse; Constance Fahnestock, Librarian of the Huntington Historical Society who located some unusual bits of Whitmania; Helen Everitt for her continuing encouragement and to Bertha Hanson and Lorraine Rosmarin who typed the manuscript.

Contents

Introduction 5

1 The Poet's Birthplace 7

2 The Whitman and Van Velsor Families 12

3 The Whitmans Move to Brooklyn 20

4 Early Days in Brooklyn 24

5 Walt Leaves School 31

6 The Young Schoolteacher 36

7 The Long Islander 43

8 Part-Time Journalist 54

9 Teaching Again 60

10 Woodbury and Whitestone 63

11 The Brooklyn Daily Eagle 67

12 The Freeman 72

13 Builder and Businessman 75

14 A Visit to West Hills 78

15 Leaves of Grass 81

16   The Brooklyn *Times* 87

17   Visits to Eastern Long Island 90

18   Last Days in Brooklyn 99

19   Aged Poet in Huntington 103

20   Long Island Honors Its Poet 108

Appendix
Notes and References 115

Addresses Identified with Walt Whitman
During His Years in Brooklyn 118

Editorial Written by Walt Whitman 120

Bibliography 124

Index 127

Illustrations

A hitherto unpublished engraved portrait of
Walt Whitman. By George R. Avery . . . . *frontispiece*

following page

Louisa Van Velsor Whitman and Walter Whitman 18

The Whitman birthplace 18

Family record from the Whitman Bible 18

Whitman portrait (c. 1840) 18

The Woodbury schoolhouse 50

The Smithtown schoolhouse 50

Letter from Walt to Carlos D. Stuart
applying for employment 50

Whitman portrait from a daguerreotype (1855) 50

Whitman portrait by Matthew Brady (1862) 82

Letter to Walt Whitman from Ralph Waldo Emerson 82

WALT WHITMAN
ON LONG ISLAND

There Was A Child Went Forth

There was a child went forth every day
And the first object he looked upon, that object he became,
And that object became part of him for the day
        or a certain part of the day,
Or for many years or stretching cycles of years.
The early lilacs became part of this child,
And grass and white and red morning-glories, and white
        and red clover, and the song of the phoebe-bird,
And the third-month lambs and the sow's pink-faint litter,
        and the mare's foal and the cow's calf,
And the noisy brood of the barnyard on by the mire of the
        pond-side,
And the fish suspending themselves so curiously below there,
And the water-plants with their graceful flat heads, all
        became part of him.

*   *   *   *   *   *

Vehicles, teams, the heavy-planked wharves, the huge crossing
        at the ferries,
The village on the highland seen from afar at sunset,
        the river between,
Shadows, aureola and mist, the light falling on roofs and gables
        of white or brown two miles off,
The schooner near by sleepily dropping down the tide,
        the little boat slack-tow'd astern,
The hurrying tumbling waves, quick-broken crests, slapping,
The strata of colored clouds, the long bar of maroon-tint away
        solitary by itself, the spread of purity
        it lies motionless in,
The horizon's edge, the flying sea-crow, the fragrance of
        salt marsh and shore mud,
These became part of that child who went forth every day,
        and who now goes, and will always go forth
        every day.

Introduction

In what has been described as the most significant letter in American literature, namely that written by Ralph Waldo Emerson to Walt Whitman on July 21, 1855, appear the familiar words: "I greet you at the beginning of a great career, which yet must have had a long foreground somewhere. . . ."

It has been the intent of the author to search out and piece together, insofar as is possible, this "long foreground"; to cull from the many available sources, the references to Whitman's life and activities on Long Island, to present them in some sort of sequence and in the context of the time during which he lived and worked there and roamed about the highways.

Whitman himself acknowledges often in his writings the importance of his early years, of his impressions and "absorbtions" of the soil and the sea and the people of Long Island.

"The successive growth stages of my infancy, childhood, youth and manhood were all pass'd on Long Island, which I sometimes feel as if I had incorporated . . .," he wrote.

Settings for the stories Whitman wrote in his early years are typical Long Island scenes, familiar to the rural and village residents of that time. In "Wild Frank's Return," the solitary traveler came up to "the quaint, low-roofed village tavern, opened its half-door and entered", and the tavern bears a close resemblance to the old Peace and Plenty Inn, operated by the Chichesters of West Hills. The action in another story, "The Last Loyalist," takes place "on a large and fertile neck of land that juts out into the Sound, stretching to the east of New York City." And ". . . that blackish gray color which belongs to old wooden houses that had never been painted . . ." the rickety gate, the short path bordered by carrot beds, beets, and other vegetables,

5

described in "The Child and the Profligate," might apply to many a Long Island farmhouse.

William O'Connor, a friend and admirer of Whitman, who wrote "The Good Gray Poet," once wrote that no one can ever really get at Walt Whitman's poems, their finest lights and shades, until he has visited and familiarized himself with the freshness and "the sea-beauty of this rugged island."

In his last years in Camden, New Jersey, Whitman urged two distinguished English visitors, Dr. J. Johnston and J. W. Wallace, to go to Long Island and see for themselves the sources of his inspiration.

One could not drive from east to west, from north to south, or diagonally across Long Island without crossing Whitman's path, probably many times. There are few stretches of beach or bay, ocean or sound, where he has not walked or sat to meditate.

Admittedly, there is little chance of saying anything new about Walt Whitman on Long Island, but what has been said can be assembled in one place; it can be made more accessible to anyone who might want to examine this "foreground" of his life. If, perhaps, there seems to be too little space devoted to Whitman's career as a journalist and the years of his intense involvement in politics while he was in Brooklyn, it is because these activities have already been adequately covered elsewhere.

It is hoped that from among the readers of this book there will be a few whose interest in Walt Whitman, as one of the most fascinating figures in Long Island history, will lead to a love and appreciation of Whitman the Poet, for this was the route taken by the author.

1

The Poet's Birthplace

The life of Walt Whitman, world famous poet, philosopher, and humanitarian, began in a simple frame farmhouse in that section of Huntington, Long Island, known as West Hills. The small shingled home was built by the poet's father, Walter, in meadowland just below the large ancestral farm that had originally belonged to pioneer Joseph Whitman.

It is not known exactly when Mr. Whitman began work on his house but it was ready for occupancy by Walter and his bride Louisa Van Velsor whom he married in 1816. Three children were born to them there.

The second child, Walter Junior, arrived on May 31, 1819. May, "the fifth month," as Walt loved to call it, is a perfect time in West Hills.

The pageant of spring ends in a climax of blossoming and bird song and fragrance. In mid-May the upper slopes of nearby Jayne's Hill gleam white with dogwood blooms set against the dark pillars of red cedar. Along the sandy path to the clearing on top, the tender green leaves of sapling birches shimmer in the sunlight and the huckleberry buds are near bursting.

In late May waves of pink laurel blossoms seem to flow down the lower slopes of the hill through the speckled shade to the lane below. On the edge of the woods the little brackish ponds ring with the shrill chatter of frogs.

Around the Whitman farmhouse lavender lilacs bloom, filling the air with heavy fragrance. In a nearby pasture young lambs butt each other and cavort about, tossing their little tails high in the air, and the chickens poke lazily around the barnyard, close to the pen where a fat sow is rooting.

From a distant field comes the clear, cool call of the meadowlark, pure as the crystal water from the Mountain Mist Spring not far away.

As May in West Hills was truly a beautiful month in which to be born, so was 1819 a good year, for it was a time of peace in the life of young America.

The second war with the British was well over and the boundaries with Canada had been established. The administration of James Monroe, who was then President, was sometimes known as "the era of good feeling."

Now, all the ingenuity and energy of the young country could be spent in developing its industry and commerce, in expanding westward. The Erie Canal was under construction and would soon be completed.

The future was almost unlimited for those hardy men and women who dared to strike out in new directions, for those willing to work.

Long Island for the most part was an expanse of flat farmland that stretched out from Flatbush eastward toward the twin tails of this fish-shaped island which the Indians had named Paumanok.

Heavily wooded sections bordered the northern shore and patches of scrub pine flourished in the east central regions of the island, where the soil was too poor for farming. A cluster of hills rose in the center of Paumanok a few miles east of Hicksville to form a sort of backbone, that extended toward Commack. These West Hills, as they were called, abounded in virgin timber: tall oaks and walnuts, and groves of chestnut and locust.

An old post road threaded its way down the center of the island, across the western plains, through the West Hills and on east to Greenport and Orient, originally named Oyster Pond. Once an Indian trail, this later was the route taken by the stage coaches that transported Long Islanders from place to place to transact their business or visit their relatives.

It is recorded that the stage coach left Jamaica at 10:30 one day and reached Oyster Pond at 6:00 p.m. the next day, stopping at one of the inns spaced along the road for the convenience of the travelers.

Smaller roads—some hard and dusty in summer and full of muddy ruts in winter and spring, others mere sandy lanes—crossed and crisscrossed the island from south to north, connecting the farm settlements with the villages that had sprung up along the shores.

In the harbors and bays formed by the irregular coast line of northern Long Island, mills had been established by the early settlers.

By 1820 a woolen mill had been built in Cold Spring Harbor just west of the ponds, on the road from the harbor to Woodbury. This mill advertised in the *American Eagle,* May 12, 1825, that cash would be paid for "Merino Wool of the First Quality." Persons sending wool to the factory were cautioned, however, that "in consequences of the difficulty and expense of collecting small accounts, no credit can be given for a less sum than five dollars."

There were other mills in the village, too, grist mills to which the farmers from West Hills, Woodbury and other outlying areas brought their grain to be ground. Since Cold Spring Harbor had been designated a "port of delivery," there were also many small business enterprises that served its flourishing sea trade. All in all, it was a busy little community.

A most interesting account of farm life on Long Island in the early days of the nineteenth century appears in a book written by an Englishman named William Cobbett[1] who lived on a farm located a few miles west of Jericho. His description of the long, sunny seasons, the fertile soil, the ample harvests of fruit and vegetables, was so alluring as to tempt many an Englishman, burdened by oppressive taxes, to pull up stakes and emigrate to America.

He also provides us with some interesting facts regarding property values on Long Island at that time.

Specifying the area between thirty and sixty miles from New York, all very familiar territory to the Whitman family, Mr. Cobbett describes a productive farm: "A farm . . . with a good farmhouse, barn stables, sheds and styles," he wrote, "the land fenced into fields with posts and rails, the woodland being in the proportion of one to ten of arable land, and there being a pretty good orchard: such a farm," he says, "if the land be a good state and of average quality, is worth sixty dollars an acre."

But, he said, the rich lands on the necks and bays, with meadowland and productive orchards, with "good water carriage" were worth three times this price.

He wrote of the wild huckleberries in the woods. The wild strawberries were so abundant that scarcely anyone bothered to pick them. Cranberries could be purchased for a dollar a bushel and were flung down into the corner of a room where they could be kept for several months, the finest of food for tarts, he said.

The endless days of sun and mild weather, the sandy loam, all brought forth rich harvests of fruit unlike any he had ever known. Mr. Cobbett mentioned meeting a man going to market with a full load of pears, so full that the farmer had to put high boards on the sides of his wagon.

However, it was the farmers themselves—their tremendous energy and strength and versatility—that he admired most.

"These Americans are the best I ever saw," he said. "They mow four acres of oats, wheat, rye or barley in a day, cradle, lay it so smooth in the swarths, that it is tied up in sheaves with the greatest neatness and ease."

He confessed that their performance in the field far outstripped anything known in his native England, but defended his countrymen by saying that the American men are "tall and well built; they are bony rather than fleshy; and they live, as to food, as well as man can live."

The ability of the farm laborers to turn their hands to any task of the season's work also impressed Mr. Cobbett—the way every American laborer could use an axe, a saw, and a hammer, was as adept at rough carpentry as at mending a plough or a wagon. They were also skilled at butchering their meat for market, a matter he termed "a great convenience."

He found that the owners of the farms in America worked as hard and long as the hired mowers, another point of difference between this country and England.

Someone had told Cobbett that Elias Hicks, the fiery Quaker preacher who at that time lived about nine miles from his farm, "has this year, at seventy years of age, cradled down four acres of rye in a day."

Hicks was a boyhood friend of Walt's grandfather Whitman— they had gone together on sledding parties over the Jericho plains and joined in other youthful merrymakings. Walt's parents frequently heard Elias preach in Brooklyn when they lived there and their admiration for him was akin to hero worship.

The spirit of young America, the prevailing air of freedom, of energy and ambition, the certainty that if a man would work, he could improve his condition and enjoy the fruits of his labor, all left a lasting impression on the Englishman William Cobbett.

Here he saw that a man has a voice because he is a man and not because he happens to possess money. Here, he is not ordered to "stand and deliver twenty or thirty times in the year by the insolent agent of Bouroughmongers," as Cobbett wrote in his book, speaking of the detested tax collectors.

Thus, through the eyes of a visitor, one glimpses the quality of life in the farm country of Long Island, of its men who were independent, industrious and self-sufficient, of whom Walt Whitman would one day write: "There is not a more hospitable, upright, common-sensible race of people anywhere about than the inhabitants of the country districts on Long Island."[2]

2

The Whitman and
Van Velsor Families

Near a point in West Hills where the South Road intersected the old Post Road, later named Chichester, was the home of the poet's great-grandfather, Nehemiah Whitman, and his grandfather Jesse. A short distance from what is believed to have been the site of the original Whitman home was the "new House" where Walter Whitman, father of the poet, was born.

At the foot of the hills and slightly to the south, was a farm of some sixty acres that Walter Whitman leased and later purchased; here he built his home, sometime between 1810 and 1816.

Like so many other settlers on eastern and central Long Island, Walt Whitman's ancestors came from England to New England, filtered down through Connecticut and then across the Sound.

One. John Whitman, said to have been born in England around 1602, came to America in the *True-Love* in 1640. In his later years Walt recalled having been told that Joseph, a nephew of John Whitman, had arrived in Huntington town by way of Milford, Connecticut, sometime before 1664.

In *Specimen Days* Walt wrote, "It is quite certain that from that beginning, and from Joseph, the West Hills Whitmans and all others in Suffolk County, have since radiated, myself included."

At a town meeting on May 30, 1665, Joseph was one of two men appointed to "keep the cattell on the first week"[3] of the annual community drive of all animals "exsept work-ing oxen and Milsh Cows . . ." out to Horse Neck. In 1679 he is mentioned as one of three arbitrators in a real estate dispute.

On June 11, 1679, Joseph Whitman was ordered to appear in court by the governor, because as "late Constable" of the

Town he had permitted a sloop to trade in "your parts" and carry away passengers "contrary to acts of Parliament as well as Law & Custome of these parts. . . ."

Four years later, Joseph was appointed "leather sealer" for the town. On April 7, 1684, he was voted a grand juryman for the year; and in 1688 he was chosen a Commissioner.

By this time, Joseph Whitman had been assigned one of the ten farms laid out to settle a boundary dispute, including land that stretched from what is now known as Crab Meadow southward toward the center of the island.

Some descendants of Joseph settled in the Commack area near the Smithtown border and intermarried with the famed "Bullrider Smith" family. Many generations of Whitmans kept a store in Commack.

According to Walt, the land of the West Hills Whitmans consisted of "500 acres, all good soil, gently sloping east and south, about one tenth woods, plenty of old trees." "Rich, appleblossomed earth," he called it.

This would be the farm of Nehemiah, Walt's great-grandfather, and his wife, Phoebe White Whitman, often referred to as Sarah. This large tract of farm land, cultivated with the assistance of many slaves, brought prosperity to the Whitmans, a prosperity that did not carry over into succeeding generations who occupied the family farm.

Apart from his reputation as a successful farm manager, little is known about Nehemiah Whitman, but the same cannot be said of his colorful wife, Phoebe, about whom many legends had been passed down to young Walt. Some of these are recorded in *Specimen Days.*

In John Burroughs' *Notes,*[4] based on information provided by Walt, appears the following: "His great-grandmother on his paternal side was a large swarthy woman, who lived to be eighty-six years old. She smoked tobacco, rode on horseback like a man, managed the most vicious horse, and, becoming a widow in later life, went forth every day over the farmlands, frequently in the saddle, directing the labor of her slaves, with language in which on exciting occasions, oaths were not spared."

The poet's grandfather Jesse, oldest son of Nehemiah and Phoebe, inherited the land at the death of his father in 1789 and carried on the work of farming in the Whitman tradition with his wife, Hannah Brush, whom he had married in 1775.

Although Walt never knew his grandfather, his grandmother Hannah, who lived until he was about fifteen, left a vivid impression on the young boy.

Again, in his *Notes,* John Burroughs describes Hannah as "noble, perhaps a stronger character," who lived to be quite old after rearing a family of sons.

She was "a natural lady, was in early life a school mistress," and possessed of "great solidarity of mind." He then comments that "Walt Whitman, himself, makes much of the women in his ancestry."

In his late years the poet gave a vivid description of the ancestral Whitman homestead. As he recalled, the "long, story and a half" building, "hugely timbered . . . a great smoke-canopied kitchen with vast hearth and chimney, form'd one end of the house. . . . In the house, and in food and furniture, all was rude, but substantial."[5]

The house had no carpets. There were no stoves, but rousing wood fires on the hearths provided both warmth and light on cold winter nights.

The food was simple and in good supply. Pork, poultry, beef, and all the ordinary vegetables were plentiful. The men drank cider at meals; coffee, tea, and sugar were reserved for the women.

Clothes, too, were mainly homespun and made from the wool sheared from their own flocks of sheep.

Books were scarce. When the annual copy of the almanac arrived, it was pored over and over by members of the family during the long winter evenings.

These evenings, too, were occasions when Walt's grandmother Hannah told stories that had been passed down from one generation to the next, stories of the Indians who hunted in the

West Hills, stories of the famous people who had traveled the old post road past great-grandfather Nehemiah's home and stopped overnight at the Peace and Plenty Inn.

This inn, owned by a family of Chichesters, and just a stone's throw from the Whitmans, was a famous gathering place for local residents, too, and Walt was a frequent visitor there as a boy.

Chichester's barn, just across the road from their tavern, was the scene of an annual hog-guessing contest, where neighboring farmers would test their ability to guess the weight of various specimens brought in for the occasion. This was one of the season's social events.

The children always thrilled to the stories of the occupation of Huntington by the "redcoats," of how the local patriots schemed and conspired to outwit the invaders in their nefarious schemes.

The British were everywhere in the area and few families escaped their ruthless treatment. The officers and men foraged wherever they chose, commandeering horses and cattle, robbing the farmers of their stores, and often taking possession of their homes.

Grandmother Whitman told Walt of "the most horrible excesses—enough to make one's blood boil." Even she was visited one day by a British quartermaster's deputy, who with some attendants came to her house and ordered her to get ready the parlor and "adjoin'g bedroom, for an officer of rank, in a few days." She did so, but the officer never came.[6]

The Whitman and Brush families were active in the cause of the Rebels in Suffolk County. One Major Brush, probably a relative of grandmother Whitman's, was often marked for special denunciation by the British and was finally imprisoned in New York for a time.

One of Walt's great-uncles was a lieutenant in Colonel Josiah Smith's regiment, which was engaged in the Battle of Brooklyn with such disastrous results. He died in that fateful battle.

These and other stories contributed by relatives and other West

Hills folk who gathered around the Whitman hearth livened up the bleak winter evenings for everyone. During the rest of the year there was no time for such things.

As the early English settlers had come to eastern Long Island and gradually moved westward, the Dutch had arrived first at the western end and expanded toward the east. The two settlements met near what now marks the border between Nassau and Suffolk counties.

Their first encounters were far from peaceful, but eventually the friction ceased, for after all there was enough land for everyone and farming it claimed all the energies of British and Dutch settlers alike. Then, of course, it wasn't too long before their young people were intermarrying.

One descendant of the early Dutch settlers on Long Island was Major Cornelius Van Velsor, Walt Whitman's maternal grandfather. His fertile farm lands lay about halfway between Cold Spring Harbor and the turnpike, in a section known as Woodbury. Just below the farmhouse was a brisk little stream of spring water, which wound along through the meadows into the woods and found its way into a series of ponds and eventually into Cold Spring Harbor.

The jovial, florid-faced major made weekly trips to Brooklyn with his produce in his big market wagon, accepting occasional passengers who needed transportation to or from the city.

The little Whitman boys considered it a great treat to sit on the high seat of the large canvas-covered market wagon with their grandfather. Often, in later years, Walt recalled his frequent visits to the country during his boyhood, when the family lived in Brooklyn. There can be little doubt that some of these trips were made in the market wagon with grandfather Van Velsor.

To Walt's way of thinking, his two grandmothers were both "superior women," but it is also quite apparent that he favored grandmother Amy Van Velsor. Gentle and sweet, she came from a Quaker family named Williams who were of Welsh descent. She was one of seven girls. Her only brother and her father, both sailors, were lost at sea.

Stories of the seafaring Williams family held great fascination for young Walt. It is certain that the story of "Old Salt Kossabone," as it appears in the poem by that name in *Leaves of Grass*, had been told and retold to him as a boy in the Van Velsor farmhouse.

In addition to farming, Major Van Velsor bred and raised horses; fine, blooded stock they were too. Walt's mother, Louisa, as a girl was a "daily and daring rider," he said.

When the Whitman boys were small, they were boosted up on the horses' backs and led around the barnyard. Later, when Walt was older, he said he used to ride every Saturday at the farm, which was but a few miles walk from grandfather Whitman's place in West Hills.

The Van Velsor farmhouse was a lively place in those days and left happy memories, which Walt treasured throughout his life.

Many years later, he recalled "the long, rambling, dark gray, shingle-sided house, with sheds, pens, a great barn, and much open road-space." He spoke of the copious old brook and spring; of "the vast kitchen and ample fireplace and the sitting room adjoining, the plain furniture, the meals, the house full of merry people."[7]

But the most precious memory of all was of the people, of his grandmother Amy's sweet face beneath the Quaker cap, of his grandfather the major, "jovial, red, stout, with sonorous voice and characteristic physiognomy."

During the British occupation the Van Velsors had not been immune to the ruthlessness and the arrogance of the soldiers. Whitman records the following incident.[8] A squad of British cavalry, on a raid, "strictly on their own account," came to Van Velsor's farm, went to the barn, and proceeded to take away a very fine sorrel mare. Walt's grandfather, then a young man, was restrained from going after these horse thieves by his young wife Amy and his sisters.

Just as the British soldiers were leading the mare out, the

major, or "Kell," as Walt called him, broke away from the women and managed to seize the bridle from the soldiers.

"They drew their sabres and flourished them," Walt tells us, but grandfather Van Velsor "was resolute and demanded to see their authority for press'g his horse." The swords flashed about his head; the women were in tears, expecting he would be killed. But the Major was strong and held on to the mare with all of his might. The British finally gave up and rode away without her.

The Van Velsors, like the Whitmans, had lived for many generations on the same farm. Walt knew every inch of their land, and loved it all. "For there," he said, "with all those wooded hilly, healthy surroundings, my dearest mother, Louisa Van Velsor, grew up."

After his sweet grandmother Amy died, and grandfather Van Velsor remarried, Walt never cared to visit the place very much. Somehow, all the joy was gone.

Nevertheless, the major was quite a man, and one whom Walt admired. "As to the head of the family himself," he wrote, "the old race of the Netherlands, so deeply grafted on Manhattan Island and in Kings and Queens Counties, never yielded a more marked and full Americanized specimen than Major Cornelius Van Velsor."

As farm life with its seasons and endless round of activities was firmly imprinted on the early life of Walt Whitman, so also was the life of the sea. Both the Whitman and Van Velsor farms were near enough to behold it from the high places, and "to hear in still hours the roar of the surf; the latter, after a storm, giving a peculiar sound at night."[9]

Frequently the men and women went on beach and bathing parties. There were fishing and clamming expeditions as well; and there were the occasions when the salt hay had to be cut and harvested.

As a boy, Walt often visited his Van Velsor cousins in Cold Spring Harbor, which was not much more than a mile from his grandfather's farm. Sometimes he would follow the little brook

Louisa Van Velsor Whitman and Walter Whitman

Walt Whitman's birthplace

Family Record.

Births

Walter Whitman	July 14 1789
Louisa Van Velsor	Sept 22 1795
Jesse Whitman	March 2 1818
Walt Whitman	May 31 1819
Mary Elizabeth	Feb 3 1821
Hannah Louisa	Nov 28 1823
Infant	March 12 1825
Andrew Jackson	April 7 1827
Geo: Washington	Nov 28 1829
Thos: Jefferson	July 18 1833
Edward	August 9 1835
Walter	Nov 4 1875
Mannahatta	June 9 1860
Jessie Louisa	June 17 1863

George Van Nostrand Jr	Dec 11th 1785
Fannie Seaman	March 31 1795
Ansel Van Nostrand	March 24th 1817
Mary E Van Nostrand	Feb 3d 1821
George Van Nostrand	April 25 1841
Fannie Van Nostrand	June 1, 1843
Louisa Van Nostrand	July 23 1845
Ansel Van Nostrand	August 24, 1847
Minnie Van Nostrand	Feb 1, 1851
Leander I Youngs	June 30th 1847
Tira Youngs	May 8th 1872
Ansel Youngs	Nov 6th 1874
Winnie Youngs	April 17th 1877
Vera Youngs	Sept 26 1888
David Tuthill	Jan. 7th 1870
John F Fish	Feb 20th 1840
George A Faulkner	
Una Lee Tuthill	
David Swertfager	
Walter W. Swertfager	
Natalie D Wrenbacker	
Nancy Merrill	

Marriages

Walter Whitman & Louisa Van Velsor	June 8 1816
Ansel Van Nostrand & Mary E Whitman	Jan 2 1840
Charles L Heyde & Hannah L Whitman	March 16 1852
Thos. J Whitman & Martha E Mitchell	Feb 23 1859
Geo: W Whitman & Louisa Orr Haslam	March 14 1871

George A Faulkner & Fannie Van Nostrand	
John F Fish & Louisa Van Nostrand	Jan 21st 1864
Leander I Young & Minnie Van Nostrand	Oct 18th 1871
George Van Nostrand & Sarah Hellum	
George Van Nostrand & Fannie Seaman	Aug 29, 1815
Noah Van Nostrand & Phebe Hoff	Oct 14 1860
Zora Young and David Tuthill	
Una L Tuthill Walter Swertfager	Aug 28, 1928
David Tuthill Swertfager	
Nancy Merrill	
Walter Whitman Swertfager	
Natalie D Wrenbacker	

The family record page from the Whitman Bible showing Walt Whitman's handwriting in the upper portion
(Through the courtesy of Walter Whitman Swertfager)

Perhaps the earliest known portrait (about 1840) of Walt Whitman from an unidentified clipping in the Long Island Historical Society archives

from the farm down through the woods and swamps to the place where it disappeared into the waters of the harbor.

Wandering along the edge of the salt marsh at the head of the harbor, he had seen how the graceful, great blue heron stood motionless for ever so long and then in a flash would scoop up a squirming fish and gulp it down with one or two ripples of his long gullet.

It was in Cold Spring Harbor, too, where he first saw a ship under full sail, which he described once as "the grandest sight in the world and one that had never been put into a poem." Many years later, Walt admitted to a friend that as a young man he wanted to go to sea and learn all about a ship. Here in this little seaport, the wonders, joys, and the tragedy of the sea were absorbed into his life, as indeed was everything he saw and felt and heard as a boy.

3

The Whitmans Move
To Brooklyn

Most of the Whitman men had farmed their land and no doubt the poet's father, Walter Whitman, had been expected to carry on in the family tradition. This he did, for a time. For eight years after he had married Louisa in 1816, he tended his farm, tilling the rich, loamy soil that had washed down from the hills above hundreds of years ago.

Farm life is always rigorous and demanding. The old saying, "man works from sun to sun but woman's work is never done," surely applied to Walter and Louisa Whitman.

The children had their little chores to do, but there was ample time left for other things. To young Walt, life on the farm was exciting, especially in the warm weather, when he could wander barefoot down the farm lane to the south path and across into the woods and feel the cool moss under his feet. Or he could follow the hard dirt path up to the old Whitman farm, where grandmother might be churning or smoking meat or setting a clutch of eggs under a nesting hen.

There were so many things to see and to hear—the throbbing throat of a singing bird or the startled "chip" of the fat-cheeked chipmunk as he scampered away over the leaves. He noticed how a sudden breath of south wind made waves move across the grass in the pasture just the way it rippled the surface of the pond and sent shudders through the clumps of yellow sweet flag. He observed the shiny black ants and wondered where they went when they disappeared into their little hills of crumpled earth.

In fact, all life was wonderful to the little boy Walt, who listened to the language of the wild things and pondered their mysteries. It all became forever a part of him, to appear and re-appear in the measured rhythyms of his songs.

But Mr. Walter Whitman's mind kept returning to those years in Brooklyn where as a boy of 15 he had gone as an apprentice to one of his relatives who was a carpenter and woodworker. Here he had been exposed to men of ideas, men who had been involved in the ferment that followed the Revolutionary War, men like Tom Paine.

After three years, his apprenticeship was finished and he had returned to the country to try his hand at house building in and around West Hills. Perhaps he had already decided to ask the hand of Louisa Van Velsor and wished to demonstrate his newly acquired skill by erecting his own farm home.

It is thought that he expected to secure more work of this sort, but there didn't seem to be much opportunity around West Hills. He did build for the Colyer family a house that was much larger than his own but quite similar in construction. It is also known that in winter Mr. Whitman occasionally cut wood, which he sold and transported to people in Huntington.

Either farming was not to his taste or he was not successful at it, for he decided to sell his place in the country and move his family to Brooklyn, which was beginning a time of great prosperity and expansion. Surely an experienced young carpenter like Walter Whitman would find good opportunities there to ply his trade.

Of course, he had kept in touch with the situation through his friends and his father-in-law, Major Van Velsor, who drove his stage-market wagon to Brooklyn every week. Mr. Whitman had himself gone in to investigate the prospects for work and seek out a suitable place to locate his family.

Finally the plans were laid and the day of their departure arrived. It was May 27, 1823, just three days before Walt's fourth birthday. The family rose well before dawn to gather their belongings and loaded them into the big farm wagon. Louisa got the children ready. They were stowed in among the piles of bedding, utensils, and other necessary items.

The little barefooted boys had padded their way up the well-worn path to grandmother Whitman's for the last time. Farewells had been exchanged and probably a few tears had been shed.

Being uprooted from the soil and transplanted to an unknown life in the city must not have been easy for Louisa. Perhaps the most painful part of the long journey into Brooklyn was when the family farm wagon lumbered along the turnpike near Woodbury, past the woods and the fields she had known so well and loved as a girl, the paths she had traveled on horseback.

It must have been a long and tiresome trip for all adults and children alike, but especially for Louisa, who had to tend to two restless little boys and mind the baby, Mary Elizabeth. She was then pregnant with her fourth child.

For a time, the boys found much to look at as the road passed through the plains of Jericho. There were scores of cows browsing in the open pasture, which served as a common grazing ground for all the farmers in the vicinity. There were the woodchucks near the road who sat up tall for a minute and then popped into their holes.

The air was fresh and fragrant with sun-warmed grasses from a pasture where a bobolink spiraled upward, spilling out his gurgling song, circling overhead as the wagon passed by.

May 27, 1823, was a momentous day for Walter Whitman and his growing family, marking an end and a beginning. But this date was to be remembered for quite a different reason by thousands of other citizens, for it was the day of the race between the famous Long Island-bred horse, Eclipse, and the pride of the south, a horse named Sir Henry, whose reputation for speed was spread abroad by his owners. They had no doubts about the outcome of this race.

For this great occasion, special boats were provided to ferry the fans from New York to Brooklyn. Great posters were everywhere announcing the race, which drew crowds from all around. It was reported that the carriages were three deep all the way from the ferry to the scene of the contest.

Of course, Louisa, being a true Van Velsor, had a particular interest in this event, as did the families of all Long Island horsebreeders. Since the main route to Brooklyn passed through Jamaica near the site of the Union Race Track, Louisa Whitman must have peered over in that direction with a fervent wish that the local horse would win. Probably her husband, Walter, had too many other things on his mind to take notice.

Eclipse did win a decisive victory that day. In Brooklyn, an enterprising innkeeper had engaged a rider with a fast horse to race in with the news of the contest, for the benefit of those who were not able to attend. At a specified point, signal flags were to be displayed. A white one meant an Eclipse victory and a red flag for Sir Henry.

Long before they reached their destination in Brooklyn, the Whitmans were overtaken by a line of horses and carriages returning from the race, the riders all in high spirits, because of this great performance by Eclipse.

In the city, at the sign of the white flag, celebrations commenced that would continue far into the night.

4

Early Days in Brooklyn

The Whitmans' first Brooklyn home was on Front Street, not far from the Navy Yard, the ferry docks, and the market where the farmers and fishermen from the Island brought their produce for the city dwellers.

Once the family were settled in their new home, Walter Whitman commenced his new venture as a carpenter and builder of small frame houses for working men in downtown Brooklyn, a career that was to occupy him for the next ten years.

At first they lived in rented houses. Later, Mr. Whitman bought property and tried building homes on speculation, but records show that he lost some of these for he was unable to meet the mortgage payments. Apparently his skill as a builder, and he was said to be a first-rate craftsman, was not matched by business acumen.

No doubt when Walter Whitman moved from the farm into Brooklyn, he had hoped to improve his financial condition, to provide a better living for his family. There were now four children, Hannah Louise having been born six months or so after their arrival in the city. But fortune never seem to favor this branch of the family.

They seldom occupied the same house for more than a year. Perhaps their rapidly increasing family demanded more living space. For whatever reason, records show that the Whitmans lived in ten different homes during their first ten years in the city, most of them in the same general area of Brooklyn.

The various addresses where the Whitman family is known to have lived, and other sites associated with Walt, are listed in the appendix.

In the early 1800's most of Brooklyn's population of less than

10,000 was concentrated near the river front, where the business
was transacted and ferry transportation to Manhattan was available. Stretching outward toward Flatbush and Jamaica were the
large farms, most of which still belonged to descendants of the
Dutch families who had originally settled there.

However, even in downtown Brooklyn people kept their farm
animals; cows, chickens, and pigs roamed freely around the yards
and streets. Sanitary conditions were generally poor and there
were epidemics of cholera.

Each household was required to keep its water bucket available for emergency use in a neighborhood bucket brigade, but
this gave small protection against the fires that frequently swept
through the houses and sheds, bringing tragedy in their wake.

It was in these surroundings that the little country-born Walt
Whitman was to spend his boyhood and early youth. For him,
everything was new and exciting.

The nearby river front teemed with life. There was the endless
coming and going of the ferries, the laughing and the cursing of
the sailors who gathered about the taverns; there was the clatter
of the wagons loaded with produce that the farmers brought
to market. The wagons were then lined up in rows by the wharves.

When Walt was an old man, he could still remember the
smell of the lampblack on the canvas wagon covers, a smell he
considered very obnoxious. But there were other odors, too. There
was the salty breath of the harbor and there was the strong odor
of whiskey that floated through the tavern door as the seamen and
officers from the Navy Yard passed in and out.

"I was a little child," he wrote, "but tramped freely about neighborhood and town, even then; was often petted and deadheaded
by the gatekeepers and deckhands (all such fellows are kind to
little children,) and remember the horses that seem'd to me so
queer as they trudg'd around in the central houses of the boats,
making the water power. (For it was just on the eve of the
steam engine, which was soon after introduced on the ferries)."[10]

Yes, there was much for a small boy to do in Brooklyn, much
to observe and wonder about. There were things to overhear, too,

fascinating conversations about faraway places, about adventures and heroes.

Many famous people visited Brooklyn. When Walt was a boy, he saw President Andrew Jackson with his shock of white hair and his broadbrimmed hat. But an incident that occurred during General Lafayette's visit in 1824 Walt was to recall with "pride and pleasure" all his life.

The general had been invited to the United States by President Monroe and spent many months visiting the principal cities of the twenty-four states. It was July 4 and Lafayette had agreed to lay the cornerstone for the new Apprentices' Library at the corner of Henry and Cranberry Streets.

It was a fine day. Crowds of people turned out, arrayed in their finest clothes, to see the beloved Lafayette on his last visit to the country in whose service he had so freely offered his life. They lined both sides of the route of some two miles, from the Old Ferry to the site of the new library, adults in back and children in front.

Present, too, were a few hardy veterans of the revolutionary struggle, men now white-haired and grown infirm, but wishing to honor the general who had suffered severe wounds at Brandywine and later shared in the perils and honors of the siege of Yorktown.

As the canary-colored barouche drawn by four white horses reached the corner of Henry and Cranberry Streets, the general stepped down and proceeded with the ceremonies. At some point, Lafayette reached down and lifted a little boy into his arms, and according to some reports, kissed him on the cheek. The little boy, of course, was Walt Whitman.

The significance of this incident—of having been touched by one of the nation's great heroes—had been so impressed on Walt's young mind that it was always recalled with relish as one of the high points of his childhood. Small wonder, then, that Lafayette was one of his favorite characters.

Walt Whitman's only formal education consisted of the six

years spent at the Concord Street School, where his family had enrolled him as a boy of six.

For some time during his school years, he attended Sunday School at St. Ann's Church, which seems to have been a happy experience for the boy. He marched with all the other children in the annual Sunday School parade, an event that continued to be a feature of Brooklyn life for more than a hundred years.

Whitman's description many years later of this church, with its beautiful lawns and trees, the ample structure wherein the Sunday School met, suggests that St. Ann's was patronized by some of the old wealthy families whose fine homes lined the shores of New York Harbor in the section then called Clover Hill, and now known as Brooklyn Heights. Some of the inhabitants of this area were the Pierreponts, Hicks, Montagues, Joralemons, and Remsens for whom the present streets are named.

One day the routine at Concord Street School was shattered by a violent explosion in the Navy Yard, when the ship *Fulton* was blown up at its mooring by a disgruntled sailor, with the loss of forty-three lives. The terrifying sound as it reverberated through the schoolroom was one Walt never forgot.

And he never forgot the full military funeral of the officers killed in that great catastrophe. In one of the historical essays Walt wrote many years later for the *Brooklyn Standard,* he gives this vivid description: "It was a full military and naval funeral— the sailors marching two by two, hand in hand, banners tied up and bound in black crepe, the muffled drums beating, the bugles wailing forth the mournful peals of a dead march. We remember it all—remember following the procession, boylike, from beginning to end. We remember the soldiers firing the salute over the grave. And then how everything changed with the dashing and merry jig played by the same bugles and drums, as they made their exit from the graveyard and wended rapidly home."

There is no first-hand account of Walt's experience at the Concord Street School—what the school building looked like, what subjects he studied, or the manner and quality of the instruction he received. Fortunately, a Whitman scholar, Florence Freedman, has made a careful search of old Brooklyn school records, journals, and newspapers of that period and has published her material in a volume called, *Walt Whitman Looks at the Schools*.[11]

Her research discloses some interesting items about the educational plan in use at the Concord school, adapted from a system devised by an English Quaker named Joseph Lancaster. A very rigid system it was, too, with emphasis on "rote learning." The teacher would read long statements, often with strong moral overtones, which the pupils repeated in unison.

The subjects studied were probably arithmetic, reading and writing, and geography.

The Lancastrian System employed many student monitors, thus enabling one teacher to supervise the work of a larger class than otherwise would be possible. Dr. Freedman suggests that this remoteness of pupil from teacher may explain why Whitman, whose reminiscences are filled with such vivid descriptions of other early experiences, fails to mention any of his teachers.

If his days at school were dull and unimpressive, as they may well have been to a boy who would prefer to wander around the wharves, his presence also left little impression on one of the headmasters, Benjamin B. Halleck. Although some years had passed when he was asked if he remembered a boy named Walter Whitman, Jr., Mr. Halleck could recall only that this boy was big for his age and rather clumsy but he did have a good disposition. He was surprised that Walt had gained recognition as a poet, saying, "we need never be discouraged over anyone."[12]

It is possible that something occurred during Whitman's school years to produce in him strong convictions against any form of corporal punishment, about which he later wrote so movingly. He certainly had never been a victim but he may well have been a witness to a merciless thrashing visited upon one of his schoolmates.

Even though his public school experience seems to have been unimpressive, Walt's education was surely proceeding in other areas.

His father was a man of limited education but very strong

convictions, a man who was steeped in the liberal ideas of his time, subscribing to a socialist paper called *The Free Inquirer,* published by Frances Wright and Robert Dale Owen, for whom he had great admiration. As a young apprentice in Brooklyn, Mr. Whitman had admired Tom Paine and the unorthodox Quaker preacher Elias Hicks, who had befriended Paine in his failing years. Young Walt must have been present during many conversations and debates in the home when his father's friends dropped in for an evening visit.

One boyhood event that Walt describes in detail was the time he was taken by his parents to hear Elias Hicks preach. Hicks was an early friend of Walt's grandfather; they were often partners in youthful escapades back in farming days on Long Island. As he developed his radical theology, which was to cause a division among the Quakers on Long Island, he was in great demand as a preacher and traveled extensively to deliver his sermons.

It was the latter part of 1829 and Walt was a lad of ten. He remembered his father coming home from his day's work as carpenter, tossing his armful of kindling blocks on the kitchen floor, and saying, "Come, Mother, Elias preaches tonight."

Then his mother Louisa hurried up the supper and the cleaning-up afterward, and arranged for a neighbor to stay with the younger children for an hour or two. Walt said he was allowed to go, since "I had been behaving well that day."

The meeting took place in the handsome ballroom of Morrison's Hotel in Brooklyn Heights, in full view of New York. Walt recalled that the North and East Rivers were filled with ships.

The audience included many fashionable ladies and dignitaries of Brooklyn. Names of some of those present were given by Walt as Hall, Johnson, Furman, Willoughby, and Pierrepont. A party of well-dressed women were accompanied by men in the uniform of naval officers.

On the low platform at the head of the room sat several Friends, mostly elderly, with their broadbrimmed hats and sober faces. There were also a few women in simple dress wearing Quaker bonnets.

After a long stillness, Elias Hicks arose, tall and straight, and looked around the audience with his piercing black eyes. Then, still wearing his hat, he spoke slowly but emphatically in a resonant voice the following words: "What is the chief end of man? I was told in my early youth it was to glorify God and seek and enjoy him forever."

This occasion so impressed young Walt, that he could recall the whole scene forty years later, when he wrote a short biography of Elias Hicks.[13]

5

Walt Leaves School

As time went on, things did not go well for Walter Whitman. Despite his hard work and the high quality of his workmanship, his poor head for business left him an easy mark for certain unscrupulous men with whom he transacted some of his real estate operations.

He was a stern man and was known to have a violent temper, which got out of hand on occasion. Walt said some years later that he thought his father drank heavily at times.

And Mr. Whitman strove to exert an undue parentalism, which Walt felt called upon to resent. On such occasions, Walt's mother was invariably the peacemaker.

As discouraging as things were for Walter Whitman, the burdens in the home must have been equally difficult for poor Louisa, who had to cope not only with poverty and constant illness among the children but also with overwork. Through it all her sweet, patient ways brought a measure of peace to this chaotic household and she managed somehow to keep an immaculate house.

Ample testimony to her excellence as a housekeeper is found in the letters she received later from her grown children. Some years after her husband Walter Whitman died, Louisa visited her married daughter, Hannah Heyde, in Burlington, Vermont, where she found "Han's" house in great disarray. This daughter had made an unfortunate marriage and never seemed able to cope with the problems that kept accumulating and threatened to undermine her health. Perhaps she had inherited the instability that had afflicted some of her brothers.

Louisa's visit had done much to restore Hannah to a more peaceful and orderly existence, and she surely left the home much cleaner than she had found it. In a letter Hannah begged her mother to return, promising that she would find the house tidy and spotless, if only she would come.

In March, 1848, when Walt and his younger brother Jeff were working in New Orleans and living in a boarding house, Jeff wrote to his mother, "I have never wanted your cleanliness so much before as I did at our first boarding house." Later Jeff wrote in a letter to Walt, "Mother has been wonderful foolish in cleaning house as she calls it and has overworked herself."

No doubt Louisa's life in Brooklyn was no more or less difficult than that endured by most women of her circumstances, but the patience and love with which she bore her burdens endeared her to Walt. The bond that grew up between them was strong, perhaps the more so because of the problems with the other boys.

Through a lifetime of trouble with the oldest son, Jesse, who was mentally unbalanced, Louisa Whitman had also to cope with the youngest child, Edward, who was a physical and mental cripple, and Andrew, who was very unstable.

When Andrew died at age thirty-six, after a long and agonizing illness, his widow, a girl of the streets turned beggar, seemed unable to manage her life and little family. Of course it was Louisa who helped care for them.

Such were the fortunes of Louisa Van Velsor Whitman. But her son Walt, who shared her burdens both emotional and financial as long as she lived, became her mainstay. Although she never quite understood him, she accepted him as he was. If she had known that this boy of hers would one day be considered a genius, she would have done nothing differently.

But hardship seemed only to strengthen Louisa's character. With limited physical stamina, she ministered to all who needed help, neighbors and family alike. Her ability to absorb hurts, to live without bitterness, made a deep impression on her sensitive young son Walt. Indeed, he seemed to inherit the gentle disposition of his "perfect mother" and learned from her the secret of inner peace.

When Walt was about twelve years old, his father lost the last of three small houses he had built and hoped to sell at a profit. With the family income so uncertain, and his father's health beginning to fail, Walt was obliged to quit school and go to work. It is quite likely that this change was agreeable to the boy, for school seemed to mean little to him.

It is known that Walt worked for a brief period for a doctor. He also was employed for a short time as messenger for lawyers named Clark, a father and son, who were said to have been members of St. Ann's Church where Walt had attended Sunday School.

This rather menial job as office messenger was itself of little consequence, but the time Walt spent in the Clarks' law office was to have profound implications for his future. Perhaps there was something special about the Whitman boy—a spark of curiosity or an eagerness to learn—that prompted young Mr. Clark to tutor him and provide him with a subscription to a circulating library.

From that moment on, Walt was an inveterate reader. He read and reread the classics. A book always accompanied his lunch pail to whatever work he happened to be doing. No doubt he had to be nudged a few times when it came time to quit reading and go to work.

His next job, in the printing office of the *Long Island Patriot,* at 149 Fulton Street, introduced young Walt to the fascinating world of newspaper publishing, a work he was to be associated with for many years.

Here at the *Patriot* Walt was apprenticed to an elderly gentlemen named William Hartshorne, who taught him how to set type. As they worked, Mr. Hartshorne, who had lived in Philadelphia during revolutionary times, entertained his young apprentice with anecdotes about Washington and Jefferson, as he recalled them from his early days. These tales fascinated young Whitman, whose patriotic family had instilled in him a deep reverence for these great figures.

But most important of all, here young Walt was allowed to print occasional bits he had written himself. What a thrill it was

to see how his own words seemed almost to vibrate from a page
of newsprint. Now some dreams began to form in the boy's mind,
dreams of a future time when he might sit in the editor's chair.
His self-education continued as he eagerly set about improving
his spelling and learning about proper sentence structure.

His time at the *Patriot* seems to have been thoroughly enjoyable.
There were other apprentices, among whom was a young man
named Henry Murphy, who had recently won a short-story contest
for a magazine in Philadelphia and later was a prominent figure
in Brooklyn politics. Plenty of spirited political discussions took
place in the office, often over some manuscript submitted to the
"*Pat.*"

The editor was a man named Clements, who, Walt later tells
us, always kept a horse and usually a fast one. He would drive
around New Lots, Flatlands, and Bushwick, carrying his papers
to country subscribers. This may well have provided the inspiration for Walt's practice a few years hence, when as editor of his
own *Long Islander* he "served his papers" around the countryside
with his good horse Nina.

Occasionally Walt used to go out riding with the boss, who,
he said, was very kind to "us boys." Often on Sundays he took
the apprentices to "a great old rough, fortress-looking stone
church on Joralemon Street."

Just how long Walt remained on the staff of the *Patriot* is not
known, but he began working there some time in 1831 and
probably continued well into the next year.

In one of Whitman's manuscript notebooks, he mentions
having been "at Worthington's in the summer of '32" and "went
to Spooner's in the fall of '32."

Alden Spooner was a successful businessman and prominent
citizen of Brooklyn, who edited and published the *Long Island
Star*. Born in Sag Harbor, Mr. Spooner was well known on eastern Long Island, where he had been proprietor of the *Suffolk
Gazette,* a position he had relinquished for the *Star*. The editorial policy of this weekly newspaper favored the views of the
Whig Party.

Walt's job of printer's devil for the *Star* gave further impetus to his ambition to write. Mr. Spooner's interest in the temperance movement may well have impressed the boy, for he not only abstained from spiritous liquor during his youth but wrote a temperance novel[14] a few years later, his first and final attempt with this form.

Walter Whitman's financial troubles continued to plague him and by now young Walt was sharing with his father the responsibilities of the family. An epidemic of cholera in 1832 was followed by a depression. In 1833, while Walt was still at the *Star,* his family moved back to Long Island, living in Norwich (now known as East Norwich).

Walt, however, remained in the city and finished his term as an apprentice. By now he was writing more or less regularly. Some of his pieces were published in the *Patriot,* others in a New York publication called the *Mirror.*

With his family in the country, young Walt Whitman could devote more time to reading, attending lectures, and going to the theater in New York, which he did frequently. In one of his biographies of Whitman, Gay Wilson Allen suggests that Walt may have benefited from the practice often engaged in by theaters whereby passes to performances are distributed to newspaper offices, hoping for favorable comments from such writers as might attend.

At some time during this period, Walt said he joined a debating society in Brooklyn. Now he could test his growing skill with words and ideas in the medium of public debate.

By the time he had become a journeyman printer and was qualified for more advanced work than he had been doing, he was able to find temporary employment in New York. But a depression and a very destructive fire brought hard times; jobs were hard to find. And by now Walt may have had a yearning for the country and to be with his family. In any case, he left the city in May of 1836 and joined the Whitman family, who were now living in Hempstead.

6

The Young Schoolteacher

During the lovely month of May in 1836, seventeen-year-old Walt Whitman was in Hempstead with his family. Although he had made frequent visits to his grandparents when his family lived in Brooklyn, this short interlude in the country must have been an enjoyable time for the boy. It was but a short journey to the South Shore with its salt creeks and bays and the innumerable hummock-like islands that dotted the west end of Great South Bay—places where Walt could fill his lungs with the tangy sea air and the rich fragrance of the sedge and salt marshes.

While he roamed about the countryside during these four weeks, he could review his past years in Brooklyn, years rich in excitement and experience; here too he had time to contemplate his future course. Scores of impressions of places and of people began to accumulate in the boy's mind, to be stored away for the time when he would weave them into his stories and his poems.

But there was the present to be dealt with and young Walt knew he must not remain too long with his family and impose upon their ever slender resources. No doubt he visited the office of the *Hempstead Enquirer,* offering his services as a journeyman printer, but he knew such opportunities were not easy to find.

It is quite certain that he gave little thought to applying for farm work. Although he loved his visits to the farms of his grandparents and spoke with feeling of the farm lanes and farm folk, he was never tempted to become one of them, to be tied down to the endless round of farm work. In fact his aversion to this idea became a point of contention between Walt and his father, who at one time pressed the subject so far that a strong altercation took place between them.

As far as is known, however, Walt never worked at farm labor.

Once when he was an old man, he did mention having spent a brief period working as a gardener, but just when or where this took place has never come to light.

Although his venture into schoolteaching may have been undertaken primarily as a means to an end, young Whitman entered into it with an open mind and a spirit of adventure. He had always loved children and as the most literate member of his family had no doubt been called upon to help his younger brothers with their lessons.

Education in those days seems to have been a very casual affair. Attendance of the children was irregular at best, depending on the weather and the needs of farm and home. Classes were sometimes large while the salaries of the teachers were invariably poor, offset in part by the custom of having free board and room in the homes of their pupils, a fringe benefit not always attractive.

Of this practice of "boarding 'round"—living two or three days with one family and perhaps a week with another—Walt said the experience "gives a first-rate opportunity for the study of human nature. You go from place to place, from the rich to the poor, from the pious to the atheistical . . . ."

Because country school teaching was usually an interim activity engaged in by those who had need of a rest, or who might need extra cash for some future purpose, there was little continuity in the schoolroom. Almost anyone who was willing and available could try his hand at it. Some of Walt's observations concerning the qualifications of country schoolteachers appeared in the *Star* on October 2, 1845, when he characterized them as "chance teachers, young men during college vacations, poor students, tolerably intelligent farmers, who have some months of leisure in the winter."

By 1858, when he was editor of the *Brooklyn Times,* he was even more harsh in his criticism, writing that teachers were "apt to be eccentric specimens of the masculine race—marked by some of the 'isms' and 'ologies'—offering quite a puzzle to the plain old farmers and their families."

It is quite possible that now and then schoolmaster Whitman

had himself been the object of such remarks. He could well have
been something of a puzzle to the parents of his charges, especially during his earlier positions when he was but an overgrown
boy himself trying to manage an assorted group of youngsters
in the schoolroom.

An imaginative lad, Walt learned as he went along and was always willing to apply unorthodox methods and ideas in his class-
room. Although not much older than some of his pupils, he was
an impressive figure, tall and well built, and having lived and
worked in the city, he was a cut above the farm lads who attended his one-room country schools.

Young Walt Whitman's introduction to the life of a country
school teacher took place in June, 1836, in the little village of
Norwich, Long Island, a few miles south of Oyster Bay. Having
known the Whitman family who had so recently lived in Norwich,
the local citizens may have been more willing to give young
Walt his first opportunity.

No records of that summer's teaching in Norwich have survived. Local residents believe that the little schoolhouse was
located on the south side of the North Hempstead Turnpike about
two blocks west of Oyster Bay Road.

Since Norwich was only a few miles from the old Van Velsor
farm, Walt probably visited his grandfather often. Perhaps here,
he rode horseback every Saturday, as did a character in one of
his stories, Archie Dean,[15] who had left the city because of the
great fire of 1835 to take charge of a small country school.

In August of that year, 1836, the Whitman family moved
again, this time eastward to West Babylon, where Walter took up
farming again on what was called "the old Merwin place." Sometime thereafter they were again joined by their son Walt, who
later recorded in a manuscript notebook that he kept the school
west of Babylon during the winter of 1836-37.

Since Walt's memory for dates was notably poor, this time of
his teaching, like many others, may be considered approximate.

The present Great South Bay Shopping Center was built on
the site of the Whitman farmhouse in West Babylon. Present at

the dedication of this Center on September 27, 1956, was a direct descendant of Walt Whitman's sister, Mary Elizabeth, who spent her married life in Greenport.

Local historians claim that the actual house in Babylon where the Whitmans lived was later moved to Amityville and presently exists as a wing to another house.

An interesting anecdote is told about young Walt at the time he was living and teaching in Babylon. One day as he was fishing from his boat in a lake near his home, the neighboring Carman boy chose to annoy Walt by throwing stones around his line, disturbing the peaceful surface of the water, and frightening away any fish that might have been tempted by his bait. Since this tactic brought no response, young Carman got into his own boat and began to row in circles around Walt's anchored craft.

The report states that Walt then engaged the other boy in conversation until he came close. Then young Whitman gave Carman a thrashing with his pole, warning him never again to interfere with anyone who was fishing.

The story does not end here, however. The father of the young Carman boy swore out a warrant for Walt's arrest before one Justice Jarvis of Huntington. There can be little doubt that the arrest of a local schoolmaster produced quite a furor in that area of Long Island. The case was prosecuted by General Richard Udall. Walt, pleading in his own defense, did not dispute the charge, but told the jury "he had trounced the boy for interfering with a fisherman's vested rights."

No doubt some of the men on the jury were enthusiastic fishermen. At the proper moment, the foreman of the jury, an Englishman, announced their findings—"that 'e did not 'it 'im 'ard enough,"[16] to sustain the charge. Although some attempts were made to challenge the verdict, the court records stood as rendered, much to the delight of most of the spectators.

Shortly after Whitman's death in 1892, some of the old residents of Babylon recalled their young schoolmaster as a handsome youth, broad-shouldered and muscular, who stood straight and tall. He walked with a slow, easy gait. His clothes were coarse, but always neatly kept; his low-cut collar and open shirt front revealed his robust chest.

Apparently the young teacher was able to instill in his scholars a desire to learn, seldom using the standard texts in the process. Years later, he was remembered by his former pupils as the only teacher who had tried to make pleasant the paths of learning. He was well liked by parents as well as by their children.

During his Babylon days, Walt had ample time to partake of the delights offered to young boys who live near the sea.

In the winter they went forth on the frozen ice fields of the Great South Bay with their axes, sleds, and eel spears.

Of these occasions Walt wrote in *Specimen Days,* "We would cut holes in the ice, sometimes striking quite an eel bonanza, and filling our baskets with great, fat, sweet, white-meated fellows."

In summer they went on bay parties to gather seagulls eggs, which were laid right in the sand and left to incubate in the heat of the sun. Walt was especially fond of this sport. In fact, the shores of this bay in winter and summer and "my doings there in early life, are woven all through L. of G," he wrote.

These expeditions may have compensated to some degree for the friction between him and his father, who had expected Walt to help with the work of the farm rather than to teach at the West Babylon school.

In the spring of 1837 schoolmaster Whitman was teaching in Long Swamp in a little schoolhouse that stood at the intersection of what is now Depot Road and Maplewood, a short distance south of the Long Island Railroad station at Huntington. It is doubtful that. he remained very long, for little information has turned up about his teaching there. Since Long Swamp is a short distance from West Hills where he was born, he must have made frequent trips across the fields to see his friends and relatives.

Probably Whitman's most impressive success as a teacher was achieved in Smithtown, where he had charge of the school during the fall and winter of '37 and '38. Although he was not yet 19, this was his fourth such position and he had by now acquired a measure of self-confidence that would make his work go more smoothly.

Fortunately for future generations, Dr. Katherine Molinoff, a resident of Smithtown, did careful research of this period in Whitman's career and has published her material.[17]

She located old school records indicating the size of the classes and found some of the textbooks that were used at that time. From early maps of the village, Mrs. Molinoff learned the site of the school when it was under Walt's direction and through interviews with old residents was able to discover some of the places where young Whitman had lived in Smithtown.

A letter written by a local resident who had attended this school describes the interior of the little building. Of course there was only one room. There were writing desks on three sides, all facing away from the center, where the teacher sat. At one end was a fireplace in which full-length cordwood was burned, giving off pleasant heat for those near the fire while the others shivered. The boys were required to tend the fire while it fell to the girls to keep the room swept clean.

According to the school records, Whitman was paid $72.20 for approximately five months of teaching reading, writing, arithmetic, spelling, and geography. At one time he had eighty-five pupils from ages five to fifteen.

Although "boarding 'round" among the families was the usual way of supplementing the low wage paid to the teachers, it could be a rather unhappy arrangement for an overworked teacher. Some quarters offered were miserable and the board often meager and unappetizing. Here in Smithtown Walt Whitman chose to make his own living arrangements, which allowed him more freedom of movement, for he was becoming a person of some stature in the community.

He joined the local debating society, which included two judges, a congressman, a justice of the peace, businessmen, farmers, and doctors, and soon thereafter was appointed secretary. His minutes were recorded in a notebook which has been preserved by the descendants of one of the members of the society.

The mere fact of his associating with these prominent citizens of the community as an equal suggests that Walt Whitman was no ordinary young man. No doubt he took himself very seriously and spent much time in preparing for his part in the debates.

The subjects of some of the debates concerned serious matters of the day, which, surprisingly enough, are still being argued more than a hundred years later; such timely issues as military training, vocational versus liberal education, soldiers' bonuses, imperialism, how to settle national disputes without war, and the age-old controversy about whether heredity or environment is the dominating force in the formation of a person's character.

According to the records of the debating society, Walt Whitman took part in eleven of the debates during his stay in Smithtown, his side winning six of them, with two judged to be ties.[18]

Of course Walt would take time off now and then to roam around Smithtown's scenic spots—the shores of the lovely Nissequoque River where the blue herons fed, and the great pond by Blydenburgh's mill, and the vast, marshy places filled with swamp maples.

The general store was the stopping point for the stage on its way from the city to the eastern end of the Island. It is said that at one time while teaching in Smithtown, Walt boarded in the home of Hull Conklin, one of the local drivers, and upon occasion accompanied Conklin on the driver's box. A story got around that while he was boarding here, "Walt had to stay in bed while his only shirt hung on the clothesline to dry."[19]

There is no doubt that Whitman's experience in Smithtown was rewarding in many ways. His pay was slightly better, enabling him to arrange his own living quarters, he had won recognition through his skill as a debater, and he was feeling comfortable in the company of Smithtown's elite. Now was the right time to move on, to do the thing he had dreamed about since he was an apprentice on the *Patriot*.

In the spring of 1838, Walt Whitman left Smithtown to start his own newspaper in Huntington, the town of his birth.

7

The Long Islander

"My first real venture was the *Long Islander* in my own beautiful town of Huntington," Whitman wrote in *Specimen Days*. It would take a combination of ingenuity and nerve for any nineteen-year-old boy to start publishing a weekly newspaper in a small country village. Moreover, if he had no resources of his own, and young Walt could not possibly have had any, it would require friends who had confidence in him.

He wrote, "I was encouraged to start a newspaper in the region where I was born." It would be logical to suppose that those who did the encouraging also provided the financial backing for this venture. Just who they were is not mentioned, but they might well have been gentlemen from Smithtown where young Walt had so recently demonstrated his broad range of interests and a talent for expressing his ideas.

The home of Whitman's *Long Islander* was a small building in a residence lot just north of Main Street and about a half block west of the present home of that newspaper. From his former colleagues in the city, he secured a press and an assortment of types, which were shipped out by boat to Huntington.

An outside stairway led to the loft of the little building, and it is said that a hole had to be cut in the roof to accommodate the arm of Walt's printing press.

In the year 1838 what is now the main business section of Huntington consisted of a few houses and shops sparsely strung out along a very broad street. Toward the eastern end was a little cluster of buildings where a tinker, a cobbler, and a tailor plied their trades and not far in the other direction was a little hat shop.

Next along Main Street was the old prerevolutionary structure later named "the Hewett House," and just beyond was the home of Mrs. Ketcham, also one of the oldest in that part of the village. Finally, toward the west, was the farm of Jesse Conklin at the corner of Woodchuck Hollow, now called Woodbury Avenue. For many years Mr. Conklin drove the village stage.

Behind the houses were open fields where in summer the mower swung his scythe and the tall corn rustled in the breeze. At one point on the south side of Main Street was a large pond edged with reeds and surrounded by a tangle of catbriers and alders. Here, during the spring, migrating ducks often settled for the night and mud turtles sunned themselves on the rocks by day. A grove of locust trees stood nearby.

On the other side of Main Street, just west of Whitman's printing shop, was the home of Horace Rusco. His neighbor to the east was Daniel Sammis, then there was the Methodist parsonage, and still farther down stood the little white church.

Not far down the street was Scudder's Hotel, later called the Huntington House and operated by a man named Ritter. This was a respectable inn where Walt and his friends stopped when they visited Huntington, many years later.

On a little hill in back of Walt's shop stood the strange-looking windmill that his enterprising neighbor, Mr. Sammis, had designed and erected in 1825 to saw and mill lumber. Shortly after he had finished this ingenious structure, he advertised as follows:

WIND MILL

The public are respectfully informed that the

SAW MILL

of the subscriber is now in operation where
he will keep on hand and for sale, all kinds
of wagon timbers, white oak plank and boards,
ash plank and white wood boards, oak lath,
chestnut rails and lath for picket fence,
white walnut planks for mill cogs; all kinds
of timber taken for sawing delivered at the

MILL

He will keep pine timbers for piazza columns,
and will turn them at the shortest notice also,
he will cut wood screws, and keep on hand,
turned broom-handles, at two dollars and fifty
cents a hundred.
                        Daniel Sammis
                        Huntington, Dec. 21, 1826.[20]

This unique structure, which could be seen from afar, consisted of a large wheel some fifty feet in diameter suspended
from a tall shaft around which it rotated. Between the upper and
lower rims of the wheel were braced eighteen sails, all rigged so
that they presented an edge when coming into the wind and full
face when moving before it.

This mill provided great sport for many generations of boys
in the village. On Saturdays or holidays, when there was a good
breeze, the lower rim would be lined with boys whirling around
with their legs flying outward. It was a rough ride and the lads
had to watch carefully to avoid the sails when they changed
position.

Walt Whitman never mentioned this windmill but it is certain
that some of the local boys who used to gather in the printing
shop of an evening had tried riding on this merry-go-round windmill. Its huge wheel presented a formidable sight perched up
there on the knoll and it would be strange indeed if young Walt
had not many a time gazed out of his window watching its gyra-
tions and listening to its grinding sounds.

To continue with Walt's own version of his venture, he said,
"I bought a good horse, and every week went all around the
country serving my papers, devoting one day and night to it. I
never had happier jaunts—going over to the South Side, to
Babylon, down the south road, across to Smithtown and Commack and back home."

Of those jaunts, he had happy memories as he recalled the dear
old-fashioned farmers and their wives, the stops by the hay fields,

the warm hospitality and fine dinners he enjoyed, as well as chats with the girls who happened to be there. A mental picture of the country roads and his ride through the brush remained clear in his mind when he was an old man.

No doubt he had counted on support for his *Long Islander* in Babylon where he still had many friends, as well as in Smithtown where he had so recently been schoolmaster and secretary of the debating society.

His whole circuit around the island villages was approximately thirty miles. Since at that time there was little communication between Huntington village on the north and Babylon at the southern sector of the town, Walt's paper must have served a need.

Although he said he hired some help, it is doubtful that the income from the *Long Islander* could support any extra hands for long. One of his brothers did work with him for a time, but Walt himself was editor, publisher, compositor, pressman, and printer's devil, all in one.

The young editor slept upstairs in his shop, "doing for himself" of necessity, for his subscribers often paid in potatoes and cordwood. On occasions when he had a little spare cash, he took a meal at the village inn just down Main Street from his establishment.

In the evenings the boys of the village used to gather in the printing room where Walt would tell them stories and read them some poetry, his own and that of others. To his own verses, he gave the name of "yawps," a word he seemed to like especially, for he continued to use it when referring to his early bits of writing.

Once established as an independent proprietor of his own paper, he could, when he felt like it, drop everything and engage in games and pranks with the other boys. One of them devised a game whereby a ring that was suspended from the ceiling had to be caught on a hook affixed to the wall. A pie was the reward to the winner. Walt's brother recalled having been sent down the street for a pie on several occasions.

The young editor was a familiar figure in the village, as he strolled about with his slow rolling gait, stopping to visit with anyone who had the time and inclination to enter into conversation. His walks would also take him to Cold Spring Harbor, which now supported a flourishing whaling industry. He would drop in on his Van Velsor cousins and chat with his friend, Ben Doty.

On an occasional Sunday morning, he wandered in the other direction to the old burying ground, which had been the site of a British encampment during the Revolutionary War. His grandmother had told him stories about the soldiers, of their lack of respect for the dead, of their deliberate desecration of this sacred resting place of the early settlers of Huntington, some of whom were Whitmans.

Here in the cemetery, young Walt contemplated the phenomenon of death, a subject that fascinated him; it played a prominent part in many of his early prose writings.

One of these stories, called "The Tomb Blossoms," must have been inspired by these visits to the old burying ground. It opens with a very accurate description of the little village where he published the *Long Islander,* his own beautiful Huntington.

"A pleasant, fair-sized country village—a village embosomed in trees, with old churches, one tavern, kept by a respectable widow, long, single-storied farm-houses, their roofs mossy, and their chimneys smoke-blacked—a village with much grass, and shrubbery, and no mortar nor bricks, nor pavements, nor gas— no newness: that is the place for him who wishes life in its flavor and its bloom. Until of late, my residence has been in such a place."

The narrator of the story then tells of returning to his quarters in the country inn one evening, where he took his lamp and retired. Awakening early the next morning, he arose and threw open his window. "It was a calm, bright Sabbath morning in May. The dew-drops glistened on the grass; the fragrance of the apple-blossoms which covered the trees floated up to me; and the notes of a hundred birds discoursed music to my ear."

He dressed and sallied forth to take a morning walk, sauntering slowly with his hands folded behind him, passing round the edge of the knoll, where the graves were located. On the left through the trees he could see at some distance "the ripples of our beautiful bay [Huntington Bay] and on my right, was the large and ancient field for the dead," all scenes familiar to him.

The story concerns a withered figure of a woman who appears with a basket of field flowers, which she distributes equally upon two adjoining graves because she does not know which one was that of her late husband.

This story was published in the January, 1842, edition of the *Democratic Review* and reprinted in James J. Brenton's "Voices of the Press" in 1850. Many years later it was also printed in full in the *Long Islander,* with the comment that anyone living in Huntington would immediately recognize the scenes described in the story.

Unfortunately, no copies of Whitman's *Long Islander* have survived, although a standing offer of several hundred dollars has been posted to reward anyone who could produce an authentic copy of the little paper. Of course it would contain news, local items, and some of his own "yawps." No doubt Walt borrowed heavily from other papers on Long Island, as was the custom at that time, and they in turn reprinted articles from his own "venture."

The first edition of Whitman's *Long Islander* probably made its appearance sometime in May 1838. Shortly thereafter, on June 16, the *Hempstead Enquirer* printed the following item:

> Another Newspaper in Suffolk County.—The *Long Islander* of Huntington has just made its debut, in a very graceful and easy manner. From its columns we judge that its publisher, (Mr. W. Whitman) has spared no pains to make it acceptable to the reading community. The inhabitants of Huntington have reason to congratulate themselves upon this addition to the roses in their chaplet.

No doubt some of the residents of Hempstead recalled the

family of Whitmans who had lived in their village for a time some four years earlier.

Other stories picked up by the *Enquirer* are probably typical of the local news published in Walt's weekly paper, such as the following:

June 30, 1838: Locusts.—These insects made their appearance about three weeks ago. They have remained ever since, and their delightful croaking is still to be heard occasionally.—The *Long Islander.*

Fishing.—This sport is said to be excellent the present season. A small party the other day in the bay, caught 64 blackfish, one of them weighing 6 pounds and several but little under.—The *Long Islander.*

The greatest height to which the mercury has risen, in this village, was on the 10th inst. The thermometer stood at 95. At Boston on Thursday the thermometer stood at 92.—The *Long Islander.*

July 28, 1838. Accidents.—On Saturday last, two boys, one a son of Jotham Wicks, and the other named George Ellwood, from the Connecticut shore were drowned in the harbor of Northport. They left home in a boat, and went to a neighboring place after cherries. While they were picking the fruit the tide rose and they were unable to get back to their boat. In attempting to reach it, (neither could swim) they ventured out beyond their depth and immediately sunk. The occurrence was witnessed by an individual at some distance, who gave the alarm and every exertion was made to obtain the bodies, in order that Dr. Ray, who was present, might attempt their resuscitation, but in vain; the bodies were not recovered until some hours afterward.

On the same day, a boy, aged about twelve years, employed in Jones' cotton factory, at Cold Spring, had his arm so severely mutilated, that amputation at the joint shoulder, was immediately necessary to save the little fellow's life. The operation was performed by Dr. Ray of this village, assisted by Dr. David Rogers of New York. The unfortunate sufferer endured it with a degree of manly composure and firmness that astonished those who witnessed it; he is likely to recover in a short time.—The *Long Islander.*

In Jamaica the *Long Island Democrat* reprinted a poem and a prose piece as coming from the *Long Islander,* one of August 8, 1838 and the other of October 31 in the same year.

According to Whitman's own account, everything seemed to be turning out well for him and his *Long Islander;* only his own restlessness kept him from establishing a permanent residence in Huntington. At least, this was his view, as he looked back at the experience many years later. There have been other speculations to the effect that the venture was not very successful and that his creditors were pressing him a bit. However, according to Mr. James J. Brenton, who published what is said to be the first biographical sketch of the poet, Walt sold his paper at the end of the first year.[21]

For whatever reason, the publication made its final appearance with Whitman's name on the masthead some time in the late spring of 1839. The young editor sold his horse, Nina, who had taken him on so many pleasurable jaunts around the countryside and who had occupied the lower floor of his print shop. It is said that his printing press was still in the loft of the building at the time his successor, Mr. Crowell, took over the *Long Islander.*

On July 20, 1839, the *Hempstead Enquirer,* which had announced the birth of the *Long Islander* just a year previously, now recorded the change of ownership, as follows:

> The *Long Islander.*—This paper, which was established at Huntington about a year since, and in consequence of the ills which newspapers are heir to, discontinued for a few months, has been revived by Mr. E. O. Crowell, who will now give the inhabitants of that town another opportunity to evince their desire to support a newspaper among themselves. We hope the editor may meet with success.

Vol. I, No. 1, of Mr. Crowell's *Long Islander* made its appearance on Friday, July 12, 1839, and the paper has continued without interruption up to the present time. This first issue under Mr. Crowell's direction carried the following editorial:

The Woodbury schoolhouse

The schoolhouse at Smithtown
(Photograph by Robin Graves)

Mr. Stuart,

I take the liberty of writing, to ask whether you have any sort of "opening" in your new enterprise, for services that I could render? —— I am out of regular employment, and fond of the press — and, if you would be disposed to "try it on," I should like to have an interview with you, for the purpose of seeing whether we could agree to something. — My ideas of salary are very moderate. —

Would you like a Story, of some length for your paper? Please answer through P. O.

Yours, &c Walter Whitman

Oct. 10.   106 Myrtle av. Brooklyn

A letter to Carlos C. Stuart in 1850, seeking employment

Portrait of Walt Whitman, taken from a daguerreotype, used in the
First Edition of "Leaves of Grass," 1855

To the patrons of the *Long Islander:*—

  The subscriber having become the proprietor of the establishment of the *Long Islander,* has resumed its publication, and purposes to continue it regularly and permanently in the confident expectation that the village of Huntington and the surrounding country will afford a sufficient amount of patronage to enable him to do so. He is aware of the disadvantages under which he must labor in consequence of the paper having been discontinued for some length of time, but by industry and punctuality, he hopes to be enabled to overcome these disadvantages and remove any prejudices that may exist in the minds of its late patrons. It shall be his endeavor to make the paper interesting and useful, and in politics strictly neutral, affording such information to the reader as will enable him to form correct, intelligent opinions of men and measures.

E. O. Crowell

Mention of the word "punctuality" in this introduction suggests what others have suspected—that the appearance of each issue of Walt's paper was not according to any fixed schedule, particularly toward the end, when it ceased altogether.

But allowances must be made for his youth, his temperament, and his love of wandering around the countryside and the harbors, visiting with farmers and fishermen. As he did so, he was making mental notes of characters and situations, of settings for his stories, and jotting down a word or a phrase touched off by something he saw and wished to preserve for future use.

After all, Whitman had demonstrated to himself that he could indeed start his own newspaper in the town where he was born, and he had proved to his successors that there would be sufficient patronage to warrant its continuation. He had delivered his papers by horse, as had Mr. Clements of the *Patriot,* where he had commenced his work as apprentice printer.

Until the time of the third generation of publishers after Whitman, the *Long Islander*'s founder was seldom mentioned. Following the publication of Walt's first edition of *Leaves of Grass,* Mr. George Shepard, who had assumed ownership of the paper in 1853, wrote a scathing review of the book. He had continued a poetry column in his paper, occasionally printing conventional verses by a local poet, James McKay, but Shepard wished to make it perfectly clear to his public that the present regime in no way approved of the ideas or work of that other poet, Walt Whitman.

As the time went on, and Whitman gained stature in the literary world here and abroad, the *Long Islander* began to take notice of his activities and eventually sang his praises.

In 1938, on the one-hundredth anniversary of its founding, it ran a series of articles on the history of the newspaper and gave due honor to the lanky lad who, in undertaking his "first real venture," created a living memorial that was to survive him by many years.

During the prime years of his life, Whitman probably gave little thought to his year as proprietor and editor of the country newspaper. However, while he was recuperating from his first stroke, in Camden, New Jersey he had ample time to recall his early experiences, some of which he published in *Specimen Days*. Here, under the heading "Starting Newspapers," he gives his account of the *Long Islander*.

In 1881, in company with his friend and literary executor, Dr. Maurice Bucke, Whitman visited the scenes of his boyhood and of course stopped at the office of the *Long Islander*, which was then located at the corner of New York Avenue and Main Street. It is reported that he dropped casually into the chair of the editor, who happened to be elsewhere at the moment, and apparently was content just to sit there and contemplate the changes that the years had brought to his little paper.

Now he was an old man, hoary-headed and feeble, though possessed of an ever inspiring presence and manner, which those who saw him would never forget.

Some years later, he was still thinking about his little newspaper. On December 29, 1888, the *Long Islander* notes:

We have received from our old friend, Walt Whitman, a Christmas present of his complete works, a gift which we appreciate very highly. Mr. Whitman is a grand old man with a good big heart, and while critics are debating about the quality of his poems, we advise any one who wants to have his heart touched with the poetic fire, to read his 'Ode to Lincoln!' We hope our aged friend may weather the blasts of many winters yet.

During his final years in Camden, when his paralysis confined him to his rooms, he had many visitors. To one of these, he handed a copy of the *Long Islander,* which lay on a table nearby, with the comment that he had started this paper himself when a boy.

8

Part-Time Journalist

It is not surprising that twenty-year-old Walt Whitman should become restless under the weekly routine of publishing the *Long Islander*. Once the little paper was established and the novelty had worn off, the young editor began to dream of other things. Memories of his last few years in Brooklyn kept coming to mind with ever stronger fascination.

While driving along some quiet country lane to distribute his papers, Walt would suddenly be transplanted to Brooklyn; he would hear the clanking and grinding of the ferries in their endless comings and goings; the clatter of the farm carts as they lumbered over the cobbles by the wharves. Many times, too, he had relived that wonderful evening when he had experienced his first grand opera and had seen at close range the magnificiently attired ladies and gentlemen of Brooklyn Heights.

Then he would recall the stirring political debates that had occurred in the printing shops where he had worked and this always led him to contemplate the tremendous power that emanated from the desk of a city editor. One day he was quite certain of one thing—he, Walt Whitman, wanted to occupy such a prestigious position where he could air his convictions or publish his poems or anything else he thought worthy of sharing.

Determined now to set his course in that direction, Walt journeyed to Babylon for a short visit with his family and then set out for the city. Fortified by his recent success as proprietor of the *Long Islander,* he called on his journalist friends in Brooklyn and New York, hoping he might find some work with a promising future.

When his hopes did not materialize, Whitman went to Jamaica and prevailed upon Mr. James J. Brenton, editor of the *Long*

Island Democrat, to take him on as a helper. Walt was not exactly a stranger there, since the *Democrat* had reprinted a few pieces from his *Long Islander* during its early days.

For a time, young Whitman boarded with the Brenton family, an arrangement that no doubt was considered as part compensation for the work he performed on the paper. Although this was apparently acceptable to Mr. Brenton, who always liked Walt and thought highly of his ability, the rest of the family found fault with his manners.

Even so, Walt found his wages to be quite inadequate to his needs and he turned again to teaching school. In one of his manuscript notebooks, he noted, "In Jamaica first time in the latter part of the summer of 1839. In the winter succeeding, I taught school between Jamaica and Flushing."

An article in the *Long Island Daily Press* on January 23, 1955, began, "Voices still ring across Flushing Hill where the Good Gray Poet once taught in a little schoolhouse." According to the writer, this school was the Jamaica Academy, which was then located somewhere on what is now called Parsons Boulevard. Here the young teacher received $82 for his six months' work.

That the *Press* should show a particular interest in Whitman's activities is not surprising, since it is a direct descendant of the *Long Island Democrat,* for which Walt worked as a typesetter under Mr. Brenton.

The *Democrat,* which made its first appearance in 1819, the year of Whitman's birth, later merged with the *Long Island Farmer* and eventually became the *Long Island Daily Press.*

Apparently Walt continued to live with the Brentons for a time after he began teaching, but he felt it was necessary to seek other quarters. Mrs. Brenton, a lady with a very proper upbringing, thought him uncouth and lazy and not fit to associate with her daughters. She claimed that the young man had sometimes spent two or three hours lying under an apple tree while he was supposed to be at work.

At other times in his life, the young poet had been and would be called lazy. By nature, he was a dreamer. His deep, contemplative moods could easily be misunderstood by those with a more practical turn of mind.

As Walt lay prone under the apple tree, he was quite likely brooding over the series of "Sun-Down Papers—From the Desk of a Schoolmaster," which he had been writing and soon would submit for publication.

If young Mr. Whitman was viewed with disfavor by Mrs. Brenton, he fared much better at the hands of his pupils in the school at Little Bayside, near Flushing, where he taught some months during 1839 and 1840.

One of these was a lad named Charles Roe, who many years afterward held positions of prominence in Flushing, elected supervisor in 1860 and six years later made treasurer of Queens County. He was a man whose memories of school days could be counted reliable.

Two years following Whitman's death, his close friend Horace Traubel called on Mr. Roe, hoping he might contribute something of value to the record of Whitman's early life on Long Island. It was recognized that such opportunities soon would be lost forever.

Fortunately, Mr. Roe possessed an acute memory and was able to provide an abundance of material, no doubt well beyond the expectations of Mr. Traubel. A detailed account of their conversation was published a year later as one of the "Walt Whitman Fellowship Papers."[22]

Recalling that none of his other teachers had made any such impress upon him, Mr. Roe said that schoolmaster Whitman had a "powerful and peculiar effect on me as a boy." At the close of their conversation, Roe said: "Even back in the school-days, those of us who knew him, his scholars there on Long Island, felt, somehow, without knowing why, that here was a man out of the average, who strangely attracted our respect and affection."

During his term of teaching at Little Bayside, Whitman boarded with a widow named Mrs. Powell, who lived about a mile and a half from the school, a distance that Walt walked each day, carrying his lunch basket.

On certain occasions, when the teacher and his young admirer took walks together through field or wood, the conversation invariably focused around the subjects they were observing, for Walt was always calling attention to some tree or bird or rock. Or to some unusual feature of the sky.

What sort of a teacher was young Whitman? Roe's account reveals a dignified, somewhat aloof but mature young man who seemed to know what he was about. No longer a novice at teaching, Walt had attained quite definite, if unorthodox, views about the educational process, some of which he would later elaborate upon during his career as a Brooklyn journalist.

Apparently he did not hesitate to experiment with his ideas at the Little Bayside School. One of his imaginative devices for sharpening the wits of his scholars and combining fun with learning was through playing the game of twenty questions. In fact, Roe said that almost everything that was done or said had an oblique if not direct bearing on their learning.

The unpleasant discipline of mental arithmetic was made more tolerable when the class was allowed to move to an unoccupied room for special practice.

Of the many incidents that came into class discussions, Walt always allowed plenty of time to a subject that held the attention of the seventy or eighty pupils who made up his class.

According to Mr. Roe, Walt had complete discipline in the school without being severe, but outside of class he was "a boy among boys, always free, always easy, never stiff. He took active part in games of frolic."

The normal hours of school were from eight to four, but in winter school kept only until it became so dark that no one could see. The subjects regularly taught in this primitive little district school were reading, writing, arithmetic, and grammar.

At times, it was customary in the schools to have "speaking," the practice of assigning pieces for the scholars to memorize and which they would then recite before the class. It developed later that some of the verses assigned by Whitman for these speaking exercises were his own compositions. Mrs. Powell had admitted to Roe that her boarder wrote poetry.

Upon describing this aspect of his schooling, Charles Roe was able to recite from memory one of the stanzas he had learned from a poem Whitman had called "The Fallen Angel." The accuracy of his memory in this detail would seem to underscore the value of his other recollections about schoolmaster Whitman.

One point he stressed was Walt's unusual way of handling discipline problems. If a boy was caught lying, Whitman exposed the fact in a story in which he mentioned no names but told in such a way that the guilty fellow knew who was meant.

Roe himself recalled taking a paper with names on it into an examination, although he did not refer to it. However, Whitman saw that paper. As school was being dismissed, he said he was sorry any of his scholars would do such a thing. No name was mentioned but the boy Roe never committed that offense again. And the lesson remained with him throughout his life.

There was no social activity in the small farm community of Little Bayside. Although Whitman probably spent much of his free time, such as there was, by himself, either walking or writing in his room at Mrs. Powell's, he found time to make frequent calls in the evening at the Roe home.

Walt and the elder Mr. Roe, a man of liberal views, became very friendly. Their conversations would sometimes range over the political issues of the day; at other times they would discuss books. Mr. Roe was an avid reader. These conversations must have been quite stimulating for young Whitman, for it is known that his interest in politics began to develop during his days in Queens.

What did the young teacher look like then? Mr. Roe said he was a rugged, healthy-looking fellow with clear eyes, firm lips, and a fine red color in his face. He dressed as did others of his time, in an old-style frock coat, vest, and black pants. He was always neat and clean. Roe thought at that time Walt had no beard.

A healthy young man with a hearty appetite, Walt ate simple foods and was never sick. He did not smoke or drink any liquors, spent as much time as he could out of doors walking either alone or with his young brother, who, according to Roe, was with him for a time.

It might be considered remarkable that Mr. Roe had such vivid memories of his teacher, but he implied that he and the other boys had often shared their impressions among themselves. Many had been deeply affected by Walt although they could not explain it—it was just something they felt.

From time to time, other friends and admirers of Whitman had come to Long Island, hoping to glean from the memories of his former scholars any bits that might illuminate these formative years of Walt's life. Each faint recollection added something of value, but it was Traubel's conversation with Charles Roe that has preserved the most complete picture of young Walt Whitman the schoolmaster.

9
Teaching Again

Just when Whitman quit his post in the Little Bayside School is not known, but according to an entry in his notebook, he was teaching again in February and the spring of 1840, this time in a place called Trimming Square. Among Whitman's papers now in the Feinberg Collection[23] is an entry that describes Trimming Square as a small cluster of houses on the Jamaica road, about two miles from Hempstead.

In his journal, Daniel Tredwell[24] of Hempstead locates Trimming Square near the side of an old race track, which the British officers appropriated for their own sporting events during the Revolutionary War. The name of this little community was later changed to Washington Square and, according to Tredwell, it was eventually absorbed into the property of St. Paul's School.

One may well ponder the various and frequent moves made by young Whitman—from place to place, from school to school. Of course, at the start of his teaching career, it was probably a matter of where he could find work, but later there were other considerations.

At some point and certainly by 1840, his schoolteaching was merely a means to an end, namely maintaining himself while he worked at his writing. Every change of environment would contribute its particular experience, and new scenes would prompt new themes for editorial comment and suggest ideas for stories.

However, Whitman's move from the school at Little Bayside, where things seemed to be going very well for him, to Hempstead may well have been planned for another reason. It was the *Hempstead Enquirer* that had first reprinted a few pieces from the *Long Islander,* and this paper had already begun to publish some of Walt's "Sun-Down Papers," on which he had been working since he came to Jamaica.

An ambitious young writer would certainly wish to be close at hand, to exploit every opportunity to publish his "yawps." He might even offer to help set up the type, a thing he was well qualified to do.

During February, March, and April of 1840, the *Enquirer* printed the first four of the series of "Sun-Down Papers." The next five or six appeared later in the spring in the *Long Island Democrat,* where Walt had recently worked for Mr. Brenton.

Although the subtitle Whitman gave to this series of papers was "From the Desk of a Schoolmaster," they actually covered a variety of topics, mostly unrelated to his teaching. They are the personal reflections of a serious, sensitive young man, tenuous projections of himself.

In one of the "Papers," the writer is the serious young teacher concerned about his little flock, cautioning them against the evils of intemperance and especially the use of tobacco. "Not only does the custom contribute to the discomfort of company," he wrote, "but it is, in itself, a fruitful source of ill to those who use it."

Another, written in a lighter vein, sings the praises of "that ancient and honourable fraternity" of loafers, leaving no doubt that Walt counts himself among the members. "We acknowledge no founder," he said. "There have always been loafers as they were in the beginning, are now, and ever shall be—having no material difference."

Surely Walt intended no offense to his church-going friends by this comment, but the whole piece may express his cumulative reactions to the many occasions when such epithets as "lazy" and "indolent" had been hurled at him. Probably these criticisms had hurt him deeply at times.

Among the various notes that Whitman left was one obviously intended for the beginning of a short story, as follows: "Of a summer evening, a boy fell asleep." In a subsequent entry appeared a fragment of poetry, "I am that half-grown, angry boy, fallen asleep," seemingly related in idea to that of the story.

In a "Sun-Down" paper published in the *Long Island Democrat* on September 29, 1840, Whitman boldly reveals his intention to write a book. Anticipating criticism, he wrote, "Who should be a better judge of a man's talents than the man himself?"

Then he goes on to reveal a subject he would include in his "compilations," his discovery "that it is a very dangerous thing to be rich."

He confesses, "some years ago, when my judgment was in the bud, I thought riches were very desirable things. But I have altered my mind." He then describes the poor miserable rich man, with wrinkles on his brow, worrying from day to day about his possessions.

At the time this "Paper" was published, Whitman was but a few months past twenty-one. One wonders at what point in his life on Long Island he had encountered such men as he chose to deride in this essay—men so heavily burdened by their wealth.

Whitman scholars have often said that Walt's early prose writings revealed no great talent. So with the Sun-Down Papers. But coming from a young man of limited education, one of a large family, dogged by insecurity in a hand-to-mouth sort of existence, they are of considerable interest. They represent a growth stage in the life of a sensitive youth whose head swarmed with ideas, with dreams and impressions; of one who would one day be hailed as America's greatest poet.

The fact that some of his "yawps" had found their way into print must have encouraged Walt to continue his writing, although quite evidently the rewards were not such that he could quit teaching school. He did, however, move to another scene.

10
Woodbury and Whitestone

In the summer of 1840 Whitman was back in the vicinity of his birthplace, teaching in the little schoolhouse at Woodbury, not far from the Van Velsor farm. In May of that same year his family had moved from Babylon to Dix Hills, a short distance east of the old Whitman property at West Hills.

The Woodbury schoolhouse then occupied a little knoll slightly back from the southeast cornor of Jericho Turnpike and Woodbury Avenue.

As teacher in this little school, Walt served as a summer replacement for Mr. Scudder Whitney of Woodbury, thus enabling this gentleman to take special training for surveying.

Many years afterward, Whitney remarked that young Walt Whitman must have spent most of his time writing poetry, "for the pupils had not gained a 'whit' in learning when he took them over again."[25] It is possible that at this time the young summer teacher was so engrossed in his next piece of writing that he neglected his scholars. Perhaps, too, Mr. Whitney was prejudiced, for Walt was near his home ground and farm people might well look with scorn on a young man who wrote poetry.

Another comment on Whitman's teaching came from a man named Sanford Brown, who told two English visitors that Walt had been his first teacher, most likely at the Woodbury School. "He warn't in his element," said Mr. Brown, then an old man. "He was always musin' an' writin', 'stead of 'tending to his proper duties."[26]

While in Woodbury, Walt no doubt spent many hours around Cold Spring Harbor, which was then in its heyday as a whaling port. The cooper shops bristled with activity when the ships came in from their long voyages and the tough breed of sailors filled the local taverns. Walt could never resist those hardy, brawny men that he called "the roughs."

It is quite likely, too, that the young man visited his old friends in Huntington village where he had spent nearly a year as proprietor of *The Long Islander*. And of course he would visit his own family in Dix Hills and such occasions would bring particular joy to his own dear mother.

From time to time rumors have surfaced in the area of Southold, Long Island, suggesting that Walt Whitman had once taught there in the Locust School and had been asked to leave.

In his writings Walt never mentioned having been at Southold, nor in his later life in conversations with friends, who carefully noted down every thing he had said.

Several years ago, Katherine Molinoff, who had done such a comprehensive study of Whitman's terms in the Smithtown school, became sufficiently interested in these stories to explore them.

Although Dr. Molinoff's careful research revealed no hard evidence in the form of school or other records, her interviews with some of the old residents of Southold produced a proliferation of the rumors. Stories had filtered down through family lines about some great-grandfather or great-uncle who had attended the Locust School under Whitman, and there was often a hint of some sort of difficulty.

Just when Whitman might have taught there has never been ascertained. Most of his time has been so carefully accounted for that there seem to be few gaps. Could it have been after he left Woodbury? It is known that eastern Long Island was familiar territory to him. In 1840, his older sister Mary Elizabeth had married Ansel VanNostrand and they had made their home in Greenport, just a few miles east of Southold.

This no doubt will always be a matter of conjecture. It is known that Walt Whitman, during the presidential campaign of 1840, had been deeply involved in political activities and had been designated official Democratic electioneer for Queens County. He campaigned throughout the country and again proved his effectiveness as a debater, for Jamaica, where Walt had been most active, went Democratic.

Once again Whitman turned to schoolteaching, this time in the quiet little community of Whitestone, bordering on the Sound and just a few miles north of Little Bayside. According to his own account, Walt had charge of the school there during the winter and spring of 1841.

Among his pupils at this school was a boy named John Morrell Smith, a native of Whitestone and one of the unnumbered descendants of the famous "Bull Rider" Smith of Smithtown. When he was an old man and aware of the fame of his former teacher, Smith recalled how Walt had sat writing at his desk a good part of the time and that he kept the class writing, too—a comment with a familiar ring.

Set in one of the world's busiest traffic lanes, often enveloped in smog, always tortured by deafening decibels of sound, the community of Whitestone still stands its ground. Today the dusky fumes and roaring of the jets mingle with that from the never ending stream of trucks and cars as they move around the bay and across the bridge; these marks of civilization have long since destroyed the peace and beauty of the place where Walt Whitman, in his black frock coat, sat writing at his desk in the one-room school.

Although this position in Whitestone ended Whitman's teaching career, his interest in education continued throughout his life. Looking back on this period, he referred to it as his richest experience. "The teaching is to the teacher and comes back most to him," he said.

Two of Whitman's "temples of learning," as he used to call them, are in existence today, although somewhat changed in form and function. The little Smithtown schoolhouse was moved to another site, remodeled and now serves as the office of a realtor just off Route 111. A marker indicates the site. The schoolhouse at Woodbury was rescued by a group of literary folk some time after 1927 and moved a short distance west on Jericho Turnpike, where it served for a time as a book shop. It eventually found its way to an estate near Oyster Bay and once again the voices of happy children echoed from its walls.

The little ivy-covered building said to have been used by Walt when he taught in Southold stands neglected and forlorn among other out buildings on a farm near Cutchogue.

11

The Brooklyn Daily Eagle

Although a passionate love of the sea and the soil, and the wholesome folk who toiled upon them, was deeply ingrained in Whitman's being, he had a burning ambition that he knew could never be realized if he remained in the country.

Memories of the years he had spent in New York during his mid-teens had been fermenting in his mind for some time; he imagined himself becoming one of the intellectual and literary elite and entering into the perpetual contest of ideas to test his own emerging philosophy. Instinctively he felt it was time for him to leave rural Long Island for New York City, this great mecca of culture and excitement.

He was now a young man, widely read, with some little reputation in journalistic circles on Long Island; he had taught in at least eight rural schools and was experienced in the techniques of printing.

Apparently he was successful in finding jobs, although they seemed to be of short duration, but it was a beginning and he established relationships that would be of benefit to him later on.

For the next few years he worked as a compositor and wrote free-lance articles for a number of periodicals, one being the *Democratic Review,* the leading literary journal of that time. For a few months he was editor of the *Aurora,* followed by shorter terms of editing the *Tattler,* the *Standard,* and the *Democrat,* while he lived in various boarding places in downtown New York City.

Meanwhile, the Whitman family had left Dix Hills and moved back to Brooklyn, living first on Gold Street and then in the new house Mr. Whitman had built on Prince Street, where with assistance from his son Walt he had purchased a parcel of land.

Sometime shortly thereafter, Walt Whitman, who had left Brooklyn as a lanky, overgrown boy of seventeen to become a rural schoolteacher, returned to that city as a sophisticated young man, an experienced journalist, a writer whose works had been printed in a dozen or more publications.

For reasons of his own, he had relinquished his independence to live again with his family, which in addition to his parents probably included brother Jeff, who would still be going to school, the mentally incompetent Edward, and Hannah Louise, Walt's favorite sister.

From Brooklyn he continued his free-lance writing, contributing on a regular basis to the *Star,* where he had apprenticed as a boy during the regime of Alden Spooner, and whose son Edwin was now the publisher.

Then, due to the sudden death of its editor, the *Brooklyn Eagle* found itself with no helmsman. Walt Whitman, not yet twenty-seven, was available and was fortunate enough to be selected for this position. Perhaps he had been suggested by his friend Henry Murphy, who had worked at the *Patriot* when Walt was there and now was prominent in Brooklyn politics. It is possible, too, that there were not many young men in Brooklyn at that time who could match the credentials of young Mr. Whitman.

It is certain that editing the *Eagle* was one of the most satisfying experiences of his journalistic career. Imaginative, vibrant with strong convictions about important issues of the day, and particularly about education, the young man was not yet disillusioned by the inside workings of politics as he later came to know them. He now moved in the company of such eminent men as Horace Greeley of the *Tribune,* James Gordon Bennett of the *Herald,* and William Cullen Bryant, who was then editor of the *New York Post.*

At that time the *Eagle,* a Democratic organ, was scarcely five years old. To have survived that long is said to have been something of a record for those days, when new papers appeared and disappeared in short order. The circulation of the paper was small and so was the staff. As there were no telephone or telegraph services in those days, all dispatches were carried by swift runners, for which tasks the "lantern boys" in the fire department were often engaged.

The four pages of the *Eagle* were heavily weighted with advertisements of such assorted items as patent medicines, insurance and real estate services, boarding places, and *Godey's Lady's Book*. It carried notices of temperance meetings and lectures, legal notices, schedules of the Long Island Railroad and of the arrivals and departures of ships. Of course there were news items and obituaries.

After Whitman took over as editor, the *Eagle* soon reflected his own particular interests, revealing the wide spectrum of his concerns. To the usual business columns, he added reviews of books and plays and long editorials.

Whitman's term as editor of the *Eagle,* which began in March, 1846, and continued until early in 1848, provided him with a measure of independence he had not known before. He was free to discourse on any subject he chose; he could publish his own verses and prose writings now and then; and he could, and quite obviously did, work at his own tempo, leaving the office whenever he felt like it.

Of this period in his journalistic career, Walt once said, "For two years [as editor of the *Eagle*] I had one of the pleasantest sits of my life—a good owner, good pay, and easy work and hours."[27]

According to one William H. Sutton, who began his long newspaper career as printer's devil at the *Eagle* when Whitman was editor and rose to become an editor himself, the shop was closed at 2 o'clock nearly every afternoon during the warm weather, so that he and Mr. Whitman could go down to the dock near the East River and sit on the pier's end to "loaf and invite their souls."[28]

The May 30, 1919, edition of the *Brooklyn Daily Eagle* contained a special edition honoring Walt Whitman on the one-hundredth anniversary of his birth. Among the features was a picture of Mr. Sutton, then eighty-nine years old, but still able to recall the old days when he and editor Whitman had taken time out to go swimming.

From another source came the suggestion that Whitman's work routine was indeed flexible. In an article in the *Brooklyn Eagle* of July 14, 1900, W. E. Davenport wrote, "In those days, Whitman might have been seen any fair day seated on the western brow of Fort Greene, usually with a daily paper spread out before him."

This particular spot was to Whitman hallowed ground. Always patriotic, ever conscious of those who had sacrificed their lives in the cause of freedom, he would here contemplate the gruesome events that had transpired in the vicinity of Wallabout not too many years earlier.

Following the British victory in the Battle of Brooklyn, large numbers of American prisoners were confined in the holds of prison ships moored off the Navy Yard, where their inhumane treatment marked one of the most brutal episodes in the Revolutionary War. Starvation, disease, and excess heat caused the death of some twelve thousand young men, whose bodies were left in shallow, sandy graves near Wallabout.

The sensitive Whitman was deeply moved by these tragic events, the British prison ships and the martyrdom of the youth, whose lives had been allowed to end so needlessly. Through his writings, he urged the creation of a permanent memorial to these martyrs, which he felt should be located on the highest point of old Fort Greene. Eventually a monument was erected on this very site, although Walt did not live to see his dream realized.

It is quite possible that from "the brow of Fort Greene" some of the themes for his historical articles called "Brooklyniana" may have begun to take form. In one of this series, which was published some years later in the *Brooklyn Standard* and the *Brooklyn Times,* was a detailed account of the prison ships in which Whitman scored the apparent indifference of so many to this tragic affair.[29]

As editor of the *Eagle,* Whitman naturally became involved in the political issues of the day and for a time was secretary of a political organization in Kings County. At first the politics of the *Eagle,* which had been founded as an organ of the Democratic party, were congenial to the young editor who had electioneered for the candidates of that party throughout Queens at the time he lived and worked near Jamaica.

The issue of slavery, which had for a long time been seething, began to emerge as the most critical issue of the day. The *Eagle* had given strong support to the Wilmot Proviso, which opposed the extension of slavery to the annexed territories. However, the split over this proposal divided the Democratic party and led to a compromise that Whitman could not accept. Violent disagreement between the editor and the publisher of the *Eagle* cost Whitman his job and left a residue of bitterness that became well-known among the journalists in New York and Brooklyn.

Shortly afterward, a casual encounter in New York with a gentleman from New Orleans resulted in an offer of a position on a new paper called the *Crescent,* which Mr. Whitman was quick to accept. On February 11, 1848, he and his brother Jeff embarked on the long trip to New Orleans, traveling by train, stage, and riverboat.

12

The Freeman

At the end of three months in New Orleans, the two Whitman brothers returned by a circuitous route to Brooklyn. Meanwhile, a group of men who had been working to establish a "free-soil" newspaper sought Whitman on his return and asked him to become its editor.

The first issue of the *Freeman* was also its last for a time, for on the night of September 9, 1848, occurred the disastrous fire that destroyed not only the office at 110 Orange Street but many blocks of downtown Brooklyn. However, its backers were determined to have their views represented in the press. New quarters were found, and some two months later the paper was again being published.

It is interesting that Huntington's *Long Islander* took note of this event. In the November 17, 1848, edition appeared the following:

> The *Freeman*—We are pleased to see our old friend Walt Whitman emerge from his late misfortune, with a spirit no wise daunted. His paper is before us, and displays much taste in arrangement, and unwearied efforts to sustain the principles formerly advocated. We hope, in all sincerity, that his labors may be attended with profitable results and 'The Freeman' rise like a Phoenix, from its ashes—and if his paper is not well supported, we are confident that it will not be from want of energy and ability on his part.

In his journal Daniel Tredwell, who had left his native Hempstead to enter professional life in Brooklyn, recorded a note reminding himself to apply for a position on the new daily paper to be published in Brooklyn called the *Brooklyn Freeman,* which was to be edited by young Walt Whitman, former editor of the *Eagle*.

Although the date of this entry, March 12, 1848, is obviously incorrect, for the *Freeman's* first issue was on September 9 of that year, it is possible that he became aware of its existence the following spring when it changed from a weekly to a daily newspaper. Its expansion would be attended by drives for new subscribers.

In a postscript under this same entry, Mr. Tredwell records: "Through all the incidents of a long life, the greatest surprise we ever experienced was on awakening one morning, many years subsequent to the above entry and finding Walt Whitman a humanitarian, a moralist and a great poet."[30]

In September, 1849, just a year after the *Freeman's* ill-fated first appearance, Whitman was again out of a job and had no regular employment until May, 1857, when he became editor of the *Brooklyn Times*.

That he did make at least one attempt to find remunerative work is evidenced by a letter he wrote to C. D. Stuart of Huntington, inquiring about the possibility of work on his new publication. Stuart had been editor of the *New York Sun* from 1840 to 1850. The *Long Islander* of September 27, 1850, states that "Carlos D. Stuart, Esq., late editor of the *Sun* is to establish a new daily paper in New York, the *New Yorker*."

Although it is improbable that Whitman knew Stuart personally, he may well have heard from relatives or friends in West Hills that Stuart had recently married Catherine Chichester Oakley, daughter of Zophar Brush Oakley. These names were all familiar to Walt and through the years members of their families had intermarried with the Whitmans.

This letter, the original of which is in the files of the Huntington Historical Society, reads as follows:

Mr. Stuart
    I take the liberty of writing to ask whether you have any sort of "opening" in your new enterprise for services I could

render?—I am out of regular employment and fond of the press—and, if you would be disposed to "try it on" I should like to have an interview with you for the purpose of seeing whether we could agree to something—My ideas of salary are very moderate.

Would you like a story of some length for your paper? Please answer through P.O.

Yours &c.
Walter Whitman
106 Myrtle Ave.
Brooklyn

Oct. 10

Since nothing has been recorded to show that Whitman ever worked for the *Sun,* it may be presumed that he and Stuart could not "agree to something."

Although the year in which the letter was written does not appear, it is known that the Whitmans lived at this Myrtle Avenue address from 1849 to 1851; the date of the announcement in the Huntington paper would indicate that Whitman wrote it in October, 1850.

13

Builder and Businessman

While Whitman was at the *Eagle* and for many years thereafter, he contributed toward the expenses of the Whitman family, sometimes buying shoes and clothes for the boys and various items for the household, such as coal and ice. Once he purchased a new carpet for his mother.

At some point, probably in the latter part of the 1840's, Walt began to underwrite some of the business deals made by his father and eventually took over the management of the real estate operations himself. At this he was quite successful, certainly more so than his father. He bought property and built homes and sold them, usually at a fair profit. At one time he is known to have served as contractor, employing others to do the building.

In November of 1848, Whitman purchased the lot at 106 Myrtle Avenue where, according to his notebook, he built a three-story house with space on the first floor for his print shop and book store. It was ready for occupancy the next spring.

Late in 1852, Whitman had a shop at the corner of Cumberland Street and Atlantic Avenue. Posted outside the house was a sign reading "Carpenter and Builder."[31] During the summer of that year, Walt is said to have hired out as a journeyman carpenter.

Among the "Free Inhabitants" listed in the July 27, 1850, census record for Brooklyn's 11th Ward appear the names of the Whitman family then living at the Myrtle Avenue address: "Walter, 61—Carpenter; Louisa, 54; Walter, Jr., 31—Editor; George, 20—Carpenter; Andrew, 22—Carpenter; Jefferson, 17—Printer; Edward, 15." In the column headed "Value of Real Estate Owned," there was no entry for Mr. Whitman but Walter, Jr., is shown as owning property valued at $3,000.

For a short time Whitman published a paper called *The Sales-*

man from his Myrtle Avenue Shop, no doubt one of his efforts to augment the family income. And he was writing articles more or less regularly for the *New York Post,* whose editor, William Cullen Bryant, had been favorably disposed toward Walt.

Their relationship developed into a firm friendship, which lasted until Bryant's death. They often took long walks together in the parks and, both being naturalists as well as poets, they must have found much to talk about. And Whitman heard with interest the elder poet's account of his European tour.

When Bryant died many years later, a lengthy account of his funeral was published in the *Sun* for June 15, 1878, which noted that among all the celebrities present, "The man most looked at was the white-haired poet, Walt Whitman."

Bryant, who lived in Roslyn, Long Island, from 1844 until his death in 1878, was much admired by Whitman, so much so that he thought Bryant's name should "head the list of American bards."[32]

Although Whitman continued with his political involvement for a time—he was a delegate to the Buffalo convention of the Free Soil Party in 1848—he gradually withdrew from active participation, having some doubts that the objectives he sought could be realized through the medium of politics.

In addition to his writing, there were many things to claim his interest. He was an ardent patron of the opera and he attended concerts and art galleries—he once wrote an article on the paintings of William Sidney Mount, the famous Long Island artist whom he undoubtedly knew personally.

He read widely, was fascinated by Darwin, dabbled in phrenology. He went to lectures, too, by such eminent men as Emerson, Cassius Clay, Garrison, Frederick Douglass, and Horace Mann. The eloquent Henry Ward Beecher he heard frequently, although he was rather critical of Beecher, believing he was more interested in attracting people to himself than to his ideas.

It is known that at times Whitman had given serious thought to becoming a platform orator himself, so he could speak out freely on the issues of the day, a thing he learned he could not do as editor of the *Eagle*. He even prepared himself to speak on a few topics, but as far as is known only one event materialized, a lecture he delivered on March 31, 1851, before the Brooklyn Art Union.

A complete text of this lecture was printed in the *Brooklyn Daily Advertizer* later that year. An interesting commentary printed some years afterward in the *Eagle* said of the lecture, "Its diatribe on the remarkable dress of the period will be of interest to all who knew what simplicity Whitman himself practiced in these matters until his death."[33]

During this period Walt was busy writing articles for the *Post* and the *Brooklyn Advertizer,* as well as working in his print shop, which along with the profit from his real estate investments must have enabled the Whitman family to live comfortably for a time. This was fortunate, for his father's health was failing and he was unable to contribute very much.

14

A Visit to West Hills

Believing that his time was limited, Walter Whitman wished to pay a final visit to West Hills, to look once more upon the land of his ancestors, and to see his sister Sarah Whitman Walters who was also in poor health. Walt, who accompanied his father on this trip, saw fit to record it in some detail.[34]

They traveled by train probably as far as Hicksville, where they took the stage to Woodbury, proceeded on foot along the turnpike and across lots to Colyer's, where Aunt Sarah lived with her widowed daughter Hannah.

The Colyer farm had originally belonged to Walt's grandfather Jesse, who had willed it to his three sons, Jesse, Tredwell, and Walter, and his daughter Sarah. The lovely old house on the property, which was built by Walt's father probably in 1819, still stands on Mt. Misery Road, in excellent repair.

"I plumped in the kitchen door," wrote Walt. "Aunt S., father's sister, was standing there. I knew her at once, although it is many years since I saw her, and she looked very old and bent."

Presently Hannah Colyer came in and the two women just stood there for a minute. After they had recovered from the first shock at this sudden intrusion they made the visitors feel a warm welcome.

During their three-day stay at Colyer's, the Whitmans visited old friends and a few of their relatives who were still living in the area. Among those they called on were the Van Wyck family, some of whom had kept in touch with the Whitmans while they were living in Brooklyn. Their old farm, which had been in the Van Wyck family for many generations, was a short distance west of the Colyer place.

In fact, Anna, oldest of the ten children born to Mr. and Mrs.

Theodorus Van Wyck, had boarded with the Whitmans in Brooklyn while she was employed in a tailor shop embroidering buttonholes on men's suits. The legend had been passed down through the Van Wyck family that at one time Anna and Walt had become engaged, but of course nothing came of it.[35]

Louisa Whitman, who apparently kept open house for West Hills folk, wrote in one of her letters to Walt, "Quite a number call to see me among the number was Ellen Van Wyck. She said she liked you and would like to see you. She is quite out of health she stayed and had a cup of tea. Ann Van Wyck's sister Ester I don't think you ever saw her she married a man named Baylis . . ."

It is apparent that Ann or Anna Van Wyck was well-known to Walt, as was her sister-in-law Ellen. Although there apparently was nothing to the rumored engagement between Anna and Walt, it is known that at least two other members of the Whitman family did marry Van Wycks of West Hills.

Walt and his father, of course, walked down Chichester Road to the old native place, past the weathered gray farm buildings and the house where Walter had been born, stopping now and then to ponder past days.

Some years later, old residents of West Hills still remembered this last visit of Walter Whitman to the land of his ancestors, where generations long dead had farmed the land and tended their vast orchards. One old man recalled hearing his father say, "That was old Walt Whitman and his boy. He must be going to die, for he said when he went away from here away back in the 'twenties, that he wouldn't ever come back again except just once before he died . . . Old Walt Whitman was as obstinate as they make 'em," he said, "and I guess he kept his word."[36]

As the two Whitman men passed by, an elderly lady called to her daughter to say that the old man was Louisa Van Velsor's husband. She recalled that young Walt, who took care of his father "like he was a woman," was very tall and had a nice smile.

Then they slowly climbed up the shady, myrtle-edged path to the family burying ground on the hill behind one of the old Whitman places. Among the graves, many of them unmarked, were some new ones, which had been added since Walt had last been to West Hills. The ailing Mr. Whitman must have sensed that soon he too would join his ancestors in their eternal rest here in this peaceful spot.

On the occasion of this visit to Colyer's, Walt seemed well impressed by his cousin Hannah but thought his Aunt Sarah was "indeed an original," a woman who cared nothing for dress but had a craving for money and property. Her masculine, determined mind may have been too much for John Walters who, Walt said, took to drink shortly after his marriage to Sarah Whitman.

After a separation, Sarah came to live in Brooklyn as a housekeeper, returning to Long Island a few years later with what Walt said was a singularly large sum of money. Here she settled down with her daughter Hannah Colyer and her husband Richard, where their industry and shrewdness were amply rewarded.

According to Walt's memory, the dates of this trip to West Hills were given as September 11, 12, and 13, of 1850, but there is good reason to believe it occurred two or three years later. Whitman was known to be inaccurate about such details.

Having satisfied the urge to see his native place once more, Walter Whitman returned to Brooklyn where he remained until his death in July 1855.

Walt resumed his varied activities with the usual flexible schedule, which permitted him to drop everything when he felt like it and go to Coney Island and fill his lungs with tangy ocean air. He loved to race up and down on the wet sand in his bare feet and, as he said, "declaim Homer or Shakespeare to the surf and sea-gulls by the hour."

15

Leaves of Grass

There has been much speculation as to when Whitman actually began working on his *Leaves of Grass;* some believe it was while he was editing the *Eagle,* others place the time later. Who, after all, could say at just what point in the long foreground of his life the seeds of *Leaves of Grass* actually took root? Walt himself once said that his poems had been gestated mainly on the shores of Long Island where he had been born and raised.

It became apparent at an early age that the instincts of the poet were present within him; even as a boy he had felt an urge to write a poem about the sea. When he was an apprentice on the *Patriot* and a compositor on various other journals, he had managed to include some of his own writings, youthful thoughts tentatively expressed in the accepted verse form of the day.

The time came when the themes that had been for so long yeasting within him broke away from the moorings of convention and the voice of Whitman the prophetic poet began to emerge. Prevented from effecting the political reforms he felt were so badly needed through his journalism, he sought to express through verse the convictions and insights that had been stirring within him in recent years.

On May 18, 1855, Whitman applied for a copyright for his first book, *Leaves of Grass.* The type was set up in the print shop of the Rome Brothers, with whom Whitman had become acquainted when he conducted his own printing business at 110 Myrtle Avenue. Until recent years, a plaque marked the door of the Rome shop at Fulton and Cranberry Streets.

The slender little book of ninety-five pages, its green cloth cover spread with sprigs of gold leaves, the title tooled in gold letters, each one draped in tendrils of vine, was offered to the public on July 4, 1855, a date that was to mark "the beginning of a great career" for Walt Whitman. This comment appeared in the letter Emerson wrote to him upon reading *Leaves* and is said to be the most famous letter in American literature.

Whitman, who had set up a few pages of type himself, was pleased with the appearance of the book. In order that its publication be given prompt attention, he wrote a few anonymous reviews for the press.

Having given up his housebuilding Walt could now stay at home and concentrate on perfecting his poems, doing just enough free-lance writing to pay the bills. He did very well at this, according to his brother George, who remarked with a tinge of resentment that Walt could lie in bed late in the morning while the other Whitman men went off every day to work at their menial tasks.

The family had no comprehension of what he was trying to do and consequently had little sympathy for him and his ways, least of all his mother Louisa Whitman. But she was usually the soul of tolerance and no doubt defended Walt's right to work at the things he believed in, to live his own life and in his own way.

In what was most certainly a daring departure from convention, Whitman printed his own review of *Leaves of Grass* in the first edition of his book. In it he portrays himself as an egotistical and reckless young man, as if in anticipation of the attack that would follow, to deprive the critics of some of their ammunition.

"Politeness this man has none, and regulation he has none," he says in the first paragraph. He then goes on to state his purpose, "to stamp a new type of character, namely his own, and indelibly fix it and publish it, not for a model but an illustration, for the present and future of American letters and American young men."

He describes himself as a man of reckless health and perfect body, six feet high and of straight altitude and slow movement on foot, a swimmer in the river and bay, and "a good feeder." His weight in 1855 at age thirty-six was 180 pounds.

He presents himself as one who "always dressed freely and

The Matthew Brady portrait of Walt Whitman taken in 1862

Letter from Ralph Waldo Emerson to Walt Whitman,
praising "Leaves of Grass"
(Original in the collection of Charles E. Feinberg)

your free & brave
thought. I have great
joy in it. I find herein
herself thinks said
incomparably well, as
they ought to be. I find
the courage of thickness
which to delight us,
which can inspire us.
I greet you at the be-
ginning of a great
career, which yet

happy in reading it,
as great power makes us
happy. If meets the
demand I am always
making forward (word)
the thirst of living Nature.
As if too much headwork
or too much lymph
or the temperament
were making us
broken into fragments.
Again you say &

The book advertised
in a newspaper,
that I could trust the
name as real &
available for a Post
Office. I wish to see
my benefactor, & have
felt much like striking
my tasks, & visiting New York
to pay you my respects.
R.W. Emerson.

Mr Walter Whitman.

must have had a
long foreground somewhere,
for such a start. I
rubbing my eyes a little
to see if this sunbeam
were no illusion; but
the solid sense of the book
is a sober certainty.
It has the best merits,
namely, of fortifying
& encouraging.
I did not know
until I, last night, saw

clean in strong clothes, neck open . . . countenance of swarthy transparent red, beard short and well mottled with white, hair like hay after it has been mowed in the field and lies tossed and streaked—a face of an unaffected animal—a face that absorbs the sunshine and meets savage or gentleman on equal terms."

Finally comes his prophetic conclusion. "There you have Walt Whitman," he wrote, "the begetter of a new offspring out of literature, taking with easy nonchalance the chances of its present reception, and through all misunderstandings and distrusts, the chances of its future reception."

Despite this display of bravado Whitman was so unnerved by the reception of his book that he retreated to the eastern tip of Paumanok, there to immerse himself in the elements of the sea, of the windswept space. There he would ride out the storm of his mixed emotions; he would contemplate his future course.

That he was quite capable of supporting himself had been amply demonstrated; indeed, had he continued with his real estate and building venture he might well have shared in the prosperity enjoyed by some of his friends in Brooklyn. But he knew that was not what he wanted.

One day, as he sat there gazing out at the wide expanse of water that shimmered in the warm sunlight and listened to the whisper of the waves as they gently washed the pebbles back and forth, he made a decision. He would go with his poems, he would speak boldly and freely of the things he felt so deeply, the things he believed. He would answer to no man. He would respond only to that deep, divine spirit that he believed permeated all of life.

After some days of solitary wandering along the shores, through the sandy back-paths that wound through clumps of bayberry and beach plum, Whitman returned to Brooklyn and his work, to the home that still mourned the loss of his father, who had died but a few days following the publication of *Leaves of Grass*. In addition to the apparent failure of his book, he suffered a personal loss.

The effort of years of labor, the book of "pomes," as Walt called them, had brought him little reward save, perhaps, the

letter from Emerson, for whom he had a profound admiration—
but he kept on with his writing, prose to satisfy his material
needs, poetry for his soul.

In September of 1856, Whitman published a second edition
of *Leaves of Grass,* this one a less ornate book with paper covers.
This volume, which included many new songs, was distributed
through the firm of Fowler & Wells, which had specialized in
phrenological publications.

Before too long, curious visitors began to drift over to Brooklyn, to learn what manner of man it was who had braved the
storms of criticism by publishing material that was so daring,
so unconventional. Bronson Alcott and Henry Thoreau were
among the early callers on Whitman and later Emerson himself
came.

Dressed in the casual fashion that was characteristic of him
at that time, heavy cowhide boots, striped calico jacket drawn
over his red flannel undershirt, Whitman greeted his guests in
the room he shared with one of his brothers. When he spoke,
it was very deliberately and in a deep voice. He listened intently,
his cool gray eyes questioning every word but revealing nothing
of his thoughts.

The white hair and beard that framed his face accentuated
his clear rosy complexion, that feature mentioned in every
description of his appearance, including his own.

There was a distinctive quality about Walt Whitman. There
was a sort of "presence" that people felt and responded to. They
found in him strange but fascinating contradictions, of which
Whitman himself was well aware, but which didn't bother him
at all. "Do I contradict myself?" he said, "Well then I contradict
myself."

He was pensive and friendly but quick to close the door to
any he thought were prying too deeply into his private world.
Even his detractors were aware that Whitman was no ordinary
man.

It is known that at one period in Whitman's life he had under-
gone some sort of mystical experience. Although the time of this

was never revealed, it was apparent during the decade of the 1850's that some change had taken place deep within him. It was as though some outer husk had been removed and he began to flower as one who found himself living in a new dimension.

He divested himself of all youthful ambitions to succeed, as men usually count success; he had abandoned that fastidious mode of dress that he had affected in his early days as a young editor and man of the world; he no longer carried the cane hung over his arm in one of his early photographs.

Instead, he adopted the simple, even crude, attire of the working man with whom he chose to identify and whose lives he praised in so many of his songs. He saw in them a basic reality and a beauty that he felt were smothered by the superficialities of society in the more "respectable" sectors.

He recognized that he was two people; that he could function in the social world and meet its demands but he was no longer bound to this world. He created his poems and matured his philosophy from his other self, from his own soul, for he had found within himself an identity that was real, was apart from the external shell of culture.

This discovery was so momentous to Whitman that he felt called upon to urge all others along this road to self-realization, but he made it clear that he could not help them in this. Each one must walk the road himself, he wrote; no one else can walk it for you.

In one of his "Songs of the Open Road" appears this declaration of freedom, this manifesto:

> From this hour I ordain myself loos'd of limits and imaginary lines,
> Going where I list, my own total and absolute,
> Listening to others, considering well what they say,
> Pausing, searching, receiving, contemplating,
> Gently, but with undeniable will, divesting myself of the holds that would hold me.

His feelings about the ongoingness of all life, of all creation, and his identity with it, speak through words such as, "I inhale

great draughts of space, the east and the west are mine, And
the north and the south are mine . . ."[37] And in the poem, "To
Think of Time," is that moving passage:

> I swear I think now that every thing without exception has
> an eternal soul!
> The trees have, rooted in the ground! the weeds of the sea
> have! the animals!
> I swear I think there is nothing but immortality!
> That the exquisite scheme is for it, and the nebulous float is
> for it, and the cohering is for it!
> And all preparation is for it-and identity is for it-and life
> and materials are altogether for it!

16

The Brooklyn Times

In June of 1857, Whitman was appointed editor of the *Brooklyn Times,* the paper that had published reviews of the first two editions of his poems. The publisher, George C. Bennett, was quite determined that the *Times* should surpass the *Eagle* both in circulation and reputation.

Whitman, who remained at the helm of the *Times* until sometime in January, 1859, continued to editorialize on the subjects that had interested him since his return to Brooklyn and wrote free-lance articles for the *Patriot.* Education, health, housing, better pay for wage earners, and, of course, the need for public parks. A sample of his editorials appears in the appendix.

Probably the subject he dealt with most frequently was the schools, and he ranged widely over many aspects, from the low state of teacher's pay to the need for better ventilation in the classrooms. He advocated the teaching of music in all schools. He was violently opposed to flogging. Pleading for free night schools to enable the carpenters and mechanics and stage drivers to improve their education and sharpen their minds, he spoke with convictions deriving from his own experience.

His theories, tested during his years as a country schoolteacher, found some support from those being advanced by Horace Mann, a man whom Whitman had admired after attending some of his lectures.

In one of his editorials in the *Eagle,* which Whitman had entitled, "Education—Schools Etc.," he wrote of the current practice in the schools, "Boys and girls learn 'lessons' in books, pat enough to the tongue, but vacant to the brain."

Merely sending a child to school, teaching him to read and write, was not to be confused with educating him, which in Whit-

man's view must go far beyond such basic matters. The pupils
should be encouraged to develop sharp, intelligent minds, capable
of independent thought and action; they should be imbued with
an impelling curiosity, a love of knowledge that would last long
after their school days were ended.

In another editorial, Walt cautions the youth of Brooklyn
against spending so many idle hours in barrooms and places of
"vapid, irrational Un-amusement," pointing out the great advan-
tages of spending their free time in improving their knowledge.

To Walt Whitman has gone the full credit for the establishment
of Washington Park near the site of Fort Greene, a move he had
advocated and promoted through his editorials.

As editor of the *Brooklyn Times,* Whitman's interests were
those of a more mature man, concerned with international and
national events as well as those of the Brooklyn area. He carried
personal news of literary figures in America and abroad.

Occasionally he wrote about baseball, a sport he had been
especially fond of ever since as a teacher he had joined in the
game with his boys in the schoolyards of Long Island.

His subjects revealed a growing concern for the condition of
social institutions and the plight of those whose destinies were
affected by them. He visited city hospitals and courts and wrote
about them.

He commented on a movement afoot at that time to make
Long Island a sovereign state and again expressed his hope that
the name of the new state be Paumanok, its original Indian name.

The editor of the *Times* was a familiar figure on the streets
of Brooklyn, with his high boots pulled over his pants, wearing
a dark blue jacket with a red kerchief knotted loosely about his
neck. And, of course, the ever present broadbrimmed hat.

Inside the building, he would often go upstairs to the com-
posing room, sometimes just to stroll up and down without saying
anything. At other times he would converse freely with the work-
ers, probably recalling his earlier years in the shop.

His editorial comments, of course, frequently touched on slavery,
the great issue of the day, and all of the political maneuvering

that revolved around it. And he wrote about certain religious matters in a way that caused offense among some members of the Brooklyn clergy, who brought pressure on the publisher of the *Times*. Rather than prolonging the matter, Whitman chose neither to defend his views nor retract them. Instead, he quietly resigned his position and it is said that there were no hard feelings on either side.

After his departure from the *Times*, Whitman remained in Brooklyn with his family, except for his jaunts into the country and an occasional trip to Boston where a third edition of his poems was to be published.

And, of course, he was always deeply immersed in his writing.

17

Visits To Eastern Long Island

The poet Walt Whitman drew his inspiration from the whole texture of his natural environment, from the infinitesimal to the infinite; the common kill-calf on the plains of Hicksville, the great oak on his grandfather's farm, the sweet-flag. He felt a kinship with all earth-dwelling creatures, with the wheeling galaxies of the universe, "the orchard of spheres." But he had a special affinity for the sea, the great mother of all life.

His youthful urge "to write a piece, perhaps a poem, about the seashore," was amply fulfilled during his mature years. "I was born within the sound of the sea," Whitman wrote, "and I know all the songs that the sea-shell sings." Images of the sea are woven into his songs; the cadence of some of his most magnificent lines suggests the undulating motion of the ocean's waves, of the white-crested, towering water-masses that crash upon the sand and then recede only to reform and assault again and again.

It is not strange that Whitman made so many excursions to the bays and sandy ocean shores of Long Island; no matter where he happened to be, he was always within a few hours journey to a harbor or the salt marshes of the Great South Bay.

In later years he chose the thinly settled reaches of eastern Paumanok, the twin points of Orient and Montauk, which jutted out into the Atlantic. He often recorded these trips in articles for the press; sometimes he jotted down descriptions or small incidents in his personal notebook. Many of these were published in *Specimen Days*.

Countless hours of his youth and early manhood were spent on the shores of Rockaway or Coney Island, sometimes at clam-bakes with friends, sometimes with brother Jeff. Often Walt walked the beach alone.

In one instance, he provides us with a beautiful picture of Long Island's north shore with its picturesque inlets and necks, undoubtedly describing the Cold Spring Harbor and Huntington shorelines, with which he was familiar.

One can almost smell the salt marshes and the hummocks of Great South Bay as he vividly portrays that area where he went on boating parties or had speared eels. He recalls the long history of wrecks along the miles of sand bar that forms the outer barrier of the Bay, mentioning the ship *Mexico,* which was lost off Hempstead Beach, and later the brig *Elizabeth,* which was dashed to pieces off Hampton, with a tragic loss of life, among them the brilliant young Margaret Fuller together with her husband and infant child .

Whitman tells us that of one or two of these wrecks he was "almost an observer." The *Mexico,* grounded on a sand bar in a violent storm, slowly disintegrated under the heavy pounding of the surf while men on the shore stood helplessly by, unable to reach the perishing victims. Indeed, Walt may have been one of these, for he was then teaching at Trimming Square, near Hempstead, and news of the shipwreck would have spread quickly throughout the area. Certainly his description of this terrible tragedy as it appears in his poem, "The Sleepers," has all the flavor of an eyewitness account.

Sometime during his final visit to his native Huntington in 1881, Whitman managed to include a jaunt to Far Rockaway with some companions. While they were off in deeper water in a boat, Walt took a leisurely bath and a "naked ramble as of old, on the warm-gray sands," while tossing lines of Homer into the sea breeze. He records the song of the sea as it impressed him during those delicious moments, "the sun shining, the sedge odor, the noise of the surf, the mixture of hissing and booming, the milk-white crests curling over . . ."

While working in Brooklyn, Whitman's fascination with the sea in all of its forms drew him to the wharves in the East River, where his trips on the Brooklyn Ferry were almost daily affairs. He went out with harbor pilots around lower Manhattan and he was once a guest on a private yacht to review the regatta of New York Yacht Club; he joined in boating parties along the Sound, one of which ended in a gala picnic at Glen Cove.

All these happy jaunts were alluded to in his notes and articles, but it seems clear that the rocky promontories of eastern Long Island had a particular attraction for Walt Whitman, for he made so many excursions to that area.

In the obituary Walt wrote many years later for his favorite brother Jeff, he remarked, "We would often go down summers to Peconic Bay, east end of L.I., and over to Shelter Island. I loved long rambles . . . and he carried his fowling piece. O, what happy times, weeks!"

While working for the *Brooklyn Eagle*, Walt made several trips to Greenport, where his sister Mary Elizabeth had lived since her marriage to Ansel Van Nostrand. He seemed to be especially familiar with Orient and Marion, frequently walked the distance· across the narrow peninsula between Gardiner's Bay and the Sound.

There is a legend that Whitman once stopped at the old Inn at Orient, a fashionable resort with a reputation for fine food, made famous also because of the prominent writers and artists who frequented the Inn. James Fenimore Cooper is said to have written an entire novel while staying there. Walt seldom specified where he stopped on his visits to Greenport and its environs, but he seemed to have been familiar enough with the fashionable summer resorts and their guests to write quite detailed descriptions of their behavior and their peculiarities, of which he disapproved. Although he certainly knew the Orient Inn and may well have had an opportunity to observe some of its fashionable guests, he would intentionally avoid specific references to it lest it cause embarrassment.

In one of his "Letters from Paumanok," published in the *New York Post,* Whitman expressed his high amusement at the summer visitors who worked so hard to preserve all the amenities of their city life, dressing each night for dinner, fearing to go out into the sun by day or to dampen their shoes by the dew of

evening, and always concerned lest their perfectly groomed hair
be disturbed by the sea breeze. For all the good they derived
from being at the shore, Whitman said, they might better have
remained in the city.

In the news columns of the *Long Islander* of June 23, 1852,
is an article entitled "Life on the East End of Long Island,"
which had been extracted from a longer one in the *Salesman and
L.I. Directory,* the advertising sheet Whitman published for a
short time from his print shop on Myrtle Avenue. This article
is introduced as follows: "Everything of and concerning Long
Island and Long Islanders, cannot fail to interest our readers."

Although no mention is made of Whitman's name, he undoubtedly wrote it himself. The first part of this long and somewhat
wordy piece is given over to a description of the numerous vari-
eties of fish that inhabit Peconic Bay. Likening the opening to
the eastern part of the Island to the jaws of some "prodigious
alligator," between which lies the Bay with its millions of food-
fish, he comments on the ease with which anyone of any age or
sex can catch his dinner in no time.

He then describes the faces and physiques of a band of hardy
fisher folk on Montauk Point, who slept on beds of salt hay and
ate raw salt pork seasoned with bad rum and spent their lives
out in their boats, fishing for sea bass and blues..

"One feels not a little ashamed," he wrote, "after mixing with
such tough koots of humanity, to be so particular against sleeping
in a lately scrubbed room, or a draught of wind from some chink
in the window."

As he was departing, Whitman hoped to show courtesy to
these rough men who had been so kind, but while they really
wanted a plug of tobacco, which he did not have, they were most
pleased to accept two stray numbers of the *Tribune,* which he just
happened to have in his pocket.

The articles then described the fleet of two hundred men in
a hundred skiffs, trolling for bluefish, darting back and forth
like swallows and "managed by five-score bold and expert water-
dogs, each ambitious of doing some dare-devil maneuver that

would eclipse his fellows—the sails bulging like the puffed cheeks of an alderman."

The writer says that this marine exhibition was prettier to his eyes than any New York Yacht race.

Describing the fishermen who inhabited nearby Block Island, Whitman likened their hair to a sort of seaweed, and says, "the Block Island babe makes for the shore with its first creep."

In other articles he wrote of his strolls around the shore front at Greenport, where he lodged and from which he radiated in all directions, engaging in conversation with the bluefishers as well as with "the originals I see all about me." Walt found bluefish the most delectable eating.

Describing in some detail a walk along the turnpike from Greenport to Marion, he and an unnamed companion encountered and, in typical Whitman style, engaged in conversation an old clamdigger with a hoe and basket on his arm. Dressed in faded blue trousers that were decorated with patches of many colors, this old man with his weather-beaten face and a hat to match had a pipe in his mouth and a dram too much in his stomach, according to Walt. As the clammer left on his mission Walt and his friend continued their stroll along the road, conscious of being watched from many windows by curious local people who customarily took note of any strangers in their village. Walt said that it was quite like a "public passage" for a time.

They continued on their way, stopping to rest at the bridge by an old mill. As they sat on the railing, they could look down into the clear stream that passed beneath and watch some eels as they slithered along on the bottom. Just as Walt had noticed a large blackfish swimming under the bridge and was wishing he had a hook and line, he was joined by the clamdigger, his dripping basket full of clams.

Whitman and his friend exchanged certain vital information and were discoursing on religion when their conversation was interrupted by the appearance of an old woman with a kettle in her hand.

She and the clamdigger, who greeted one another as Uncle

Dan and Aunt Rebby, discussed old times. Aunt Rebby remarked that the young folks of that time didn't have half as much fun as they did in her day, some fifty years ago.

Casual conversation with strangers was second nature to Whitman, who continued to observe that old Long Island custom of hailing everyone he met when he was an old man driving around Camden with his horse and carriage.

In one of Whitman's Brooklyniana articles he tells of an occasion when he was fishing from the dock at Greenport and had caught some nice blackfish, using fiddler crabs for bait, when he was invited to join a sailing party of young girls escorted by a young clergyman. He accepted, of course, and the sloop was loaded up with picnic baskets and passengers, which included one or two young fellows and the man who was in charge of the sloop. Lines were loosened and the wind soon filled the sails as the boat heeled over gently into the waters of Gardiner's Bay. Whitman learned that the expedition was headed for Montauk Point, one of his favorite spots.

The girls were good sailors and full of high spirits. The minister joined in the fun, laughing and telling stories with the rest of them. As for Walt, he was thrilled just to be sailing, to bend over and watch the ripples as the prow divided the water— merely "to breathe and live in that sweet air and clear sunlight" was enough.

The sloop rounded Shelter Island, passed Gardiner's Island off in the distance on their left, and later followed the shore of the Montauk peninsula. Arriving at the Point, they climbed Turtlehill to the lighthouse, whose powerful beam had shone from a point two hundred feet above sea level since 1796. In a comfortable little house a short distance down the hill lived the lightkeeper and his wife, who often accepted boarders and served meals to transients during the summer months.

Whoever had arranged the sailing party had neglected to make advance reservations for them to dine at the cottage. By the time they had finished playing their games on the shore and over the cliffs, they learned that other parties before them had consumed all the available food.

But the hungry sailors prevailed on the landlady to kill six fat pullets from her flock and provide cabbage, onions, and potatoes from the garden, with which they all proceeded down to the water, Walt bringing up the rear with a stewpan.

On the boat they improvised a table and seats with boards and barrels and ate a dinner that Walt said he would never forget, but he fails to tell just how the meal was cooked.

Meanwhile, time had gotten away from them. When they put out for home, the tide was against them and they were becalmed. As night fell, the young ones amused themselves with song and ghost tales, while Walt lay on a bearskin on the deck and without saying a word watched the new moon down in the west. Eventually, he fell asleep in his bed in the furled sail. He said he awoke many times in the night and "saw the countless armies of heaven marching stilly in the space up there . . ."

At sunrise all came to life. After a plentiful breakfast, which seemed to appear from nowhere, the sail was hoisted and the sloop was again gliding across the bay toward Greenport. As the familiar steeples and white-painted houses came nearer, the spirits of the party seemed to become more subdued. When they landed, all was tame and respectable again.

Unfortunately, no report of this unusual picnic has come from any source other than Walt himself. The frantic parents of the young girls were no doubt so relieved at their safe return that all else was soon forgotten. At that time Whitman was a Brooklyn journalist, a friendly and perhaps strange man, one whose personal magnetism always seemed to leave an imprint on all who came within his circle.

But there were other times on eastern Long Island when Whitman was alone, a solitary figure seated in a sheltered hollow of rock and sand, reading the Old and New Testaments, absorbing Shakespeare and Homer and Dante, with the sea on each side of him. It makes such a difference where one reads, he said.

Such works could be understood much better in the presence of outdoor influences.

When the first draft of *Leaves of Grass* had been completed, Whitman took it with him to Orient Point, there to reread it. But he was not satisfied with it and is said to have tossed it into the wind where it was carried out to sea.

Later, when the book everywhere raised such a storm of anger and condemnation, Walt retired to the eastern tip of the Island, there to contemplate, there to become absorbed into the mystique of the sea. He walked alone around the familiar shores and bluffs, fragrant with sweet-fern and bayberry. Once he had made that watershed decision to follow what he believed was his calling—to become the prophet-poet of democracy—the rest of his stay on eastern Long Island became one of the happiest times of his life.

Many of Whitman's most vivid poems bear the flavor of and seem almost to have been moulded by the sea, whose voice was ever whispering in his ears as he sat amid the sandhills.

Always searching for the words, the symbols that would best express his feelings, his emotional response to the various elements of the ocean's perpetual encounter with the shore, Whitman left in his *Notes and Fragments* some suggested titles for a poem on which he may have been working at the time.

Breath and Spray
Breath and Drift
Drift Leaves
Ripples and Drift
Sands and Drift
Eddies and Drift

They may have preceded his eventual choice of "Sea-Drift," the title he gave to his group of sea poems. Perhaps they were experimental phrases for that marvelous and dolorous work, "As I Ebb'd With the Ocean of Life," written at a moment when

Whitman seemed deep in despair, doubting himself, questioning the meaning of all human existence.

Among his last poems included in "Sands at Seventy" is the following:

From Montauk Point

I stand as on some mighty eagle's beak
Eastward the sea absorbing, viewing, (nothing but sea and
    sky,)
The tossing waves, the foam, the ships in the distance,
The wild unrest, the snowy curling caps—that inbound urge
    and urge of waves.
Seeking the shores forever.

To a visitor at his Camden home, who apparently was distressed to see this lover of nature confined in such mean quarters, Whitman said that all he had to do was close his eyes and go back to the woods and the meadows he loved—to the seashores of Long Island, for all these were forever a part of him.

18

Last Days in Brooklyn

The historical essays called "Brooklyniana," on which Whitman had been at work for some time, were published serially in the *Brooklyn Standard* during 1861 and 1862. As was indicated in the subtitle, "A Series of Local Articles on Past and Present," a variety of subjects was covered in the thirty-nine pieces.

The story of the early Dutch settlements in Brooklyn, a history of the Brooklyn Fire Department, the prison ship martyrs, and a variety of other topics portraying the economic and cultural life of the times were included.

A few articles described in some detail Whitman's trips on the Long Island Railroad to the eastern end of Paumonok, commenting upon the peculiar features of the countryside and the little villages along the route.

Meanwhile, the events that led to the Civil War were gathering momentum. After the shocking attack on Fort Sumter, George Whitman had enlisted in the army for a short term, believing when he left that the war would soon be over. As the situation worsened, he re-enlisted and later was reported missing following the Battle of Fredericksburg.

Of course, this caused great anguish in the family circle. Something had to be done immediately. Walt, who was the least bound by commitments, was the logical man to go to Washington to trace the movements of George's regiment and if possible gain access to the casualty records.

In this, Whitman was successful, and to his great relief learned that George was not only alive but had suffered only superficial wounds, from which he soon recovered. Returning to the field of action, George Whitman was again a casualty, this time as a prisoner of war. Confined in one of the notorious confederate prisons, he suffered terrible deprivations and might not have survived had he not been one of a group for which an exchange had been negotiated.

Through his efforts to locate George, Walt Whitman came in contact with all the gruesomeness and tragedy of war and its aftermath. Hundreds of wounded men who were pouring into Washington were accommodated in improvised hospitals in some government buildings, which were entirely unsuited for such purposes. Medical and nursing care were at best inadequate.

Moved by the plight of these wounded and dying men, many of them mere boys, Walt remained in Washington and devoted his next few years to assisting with the nursing care. More than that, he was brother, mother, and father to these suffering souls. He wrote letters to their families, and he purchased small items for his boys with money he raised through personal appeals to family and friends in Brooklyn.

Financing himself through part-time positions in various government bureaus and occasional articles for New York and Brooklyn newspapers, Whitman continued with his ministrations to the wounded, his outpouring of himself, abandoning all his own precepts concerning proper care of one's health. Overexertion and malnutrition eventually combined so to weaken his strong constitution and resistance that his health broke. He suffered from a stroke and other complications from which he never fully recovered.

Although it was not contemplated at the time, Whitman's hastily arranged trip to Washington to search for George marked the end of his life and career in Brooklyn and Long Island.

He did on several occasions return to visit his friends and family; in November of 1864 he came, no doubt at the insistence of his family, to share in the decision of what to do about Jesse, their oldest brother, who had become so violent at times that they feared for their mother's safety.

During this visit it was agreed to have Jesse Whitman committed to the Kings County Asylum in Brooklyn, where he remained until his death. The painful responsibility of signing the papers fell to Walt, the oldest remaining son.

In March of 1865, when the Whitman family received word that George had been released from the Confederate prison where he had been detained, and would be coming home to Brooklyn, Walt was granted a two-week's leave from his government position so he could join the family on this wonderful occasion.

All the Whitmans had received the news of George's good fortune with a mixed sense of wonder and disbelief—their son and brother, who had been wounded, then taken prisoner, would be coming home at last. What a wonderful family reunion would take place that Easter weekend!

But it was not to be. News of the tragic event that took place on Good Friday, the assassination of President Lincoln, reached the Whitman home the day after it happened. At first stunned, then overwhelmed by deep depression, the family were unable to eat or to speak. Time seemed to stand still, framing forever in their minds each small detail of the scene that had been so familiar and now seemed so strange—the room, the table set with food which no one now cared to taste, the kitchen door, the familiar lilac bush standing just outside. Walt noted how the bush was just putting forth its fragrant new leaves, how the flower buds were fattening and showing color. There were lilacs around the kitchen at his birthplace and around grandfather Whitman's farmhouse.

The lilac became a symbol of this moment of mourning and heartbreak. It inspired one of Whitman's finest poems, which he wrote shortly after returning to Washington to commemorate the death of President Lincoln. The title, "When Lilacs Last in the Dooryard Bloom'd."

Once, when he had a serious spell of illness, Whitman came back to Brooklyn to recuperate, but within a short time he felt well enough to return to Washington.

So ends Whitman's life in the Brooklyn he had served for his twenty years as journalist, where he endured controversy and harrassment, where he had risen from an unpromising background to become a poet of great promise.

This great lumbering figure in colorful but unconventional dress would no longer be seen wandering around the streets of Brooklyn or riding beside the operators of the street cars or in the pilot houses of the Brooklyn ferries. He would be missed by his many friends, who numbered in the hundreds from the "roughs" to the cultured; he would even be missed by his detractors, who drew satisfaction from attacking him. And Whitman would never forget Brooklyn and his beloved Paumonok.

In Brooklyn, Whitman had come of age. He had availed himself of all the cultural opportunities in the city—he had a special fondness for Italian opera—he had heard the most famous musical artists of the day, tasted for a time the Bohemian life in New York, dabbled in politics, edited two leading newspapers, and published his *Leaves of Grass*.

In later years in Camden, he took satisfaction from recalling his rich and varied experience in Brooklyn, his encounters with the prominent figures in history and literature. He had seen President Jackson and General Lafayette, had talked with Aaron Burr; he had known well William Cullen Bryant. And there were the many distinguished men who had called on him in Brooklyn—Emerson, Thoreau, Alcott, and many others.

He might have returned to enjoy the adulation that was beginning to come from abroad, thus enhancing his status at home, but Walt Whitman was not the same man who had left Brooklyn. His Washington experience had wrought a deep change in him; the suffering he had endured reflected those changes in his face and his poetry. In a sense he had outgrown Brooklyn.

As his health declined, Walt made his home in Camden, New Jersey, where his brother George had settled after his military career was finished. Their mother, Louisa Whitman, ended her days there with her two sons. In Camden, the poet purchased a home on Mickle Street, where he received his friends from America and abroad, and basked in the fame he had now achieved.

19

Aged Poet at Huntington

As his father had done before him, Walt Whitman paid a final visit to his native place and a few of his favorite haunts on Long Island. Although he particularly wanted to identify his birthplace, he also yearned to explore once more the picturesque regions of Huntington and Cold Spring Harbor and to see again the magnificent view from the top of Jayne's Hill, the highest point on Long Island.

In late July of 1881, Whitman and his close friend, Dr. R. M. Bucke of Ontario, Canada, journeyed to Huntington, where they put up at the Huntington House, just a short block east of the small barn where Walt had published his *Long Islander*. From here they spent some days touring around the area, probably pausing the longest in the vicinity of West Hills. They were driven and escorted by a young man named Fred Galow, who, it is reported, was presented with a copy of *Leaves of Grass* at the end of Whitman's visit.

One of their first calls in West Hills was at the old Whitman homestead, then occupied by Philo Place. From the upland they could look to the east and south over the beautiful farmlands of his grandfather, and a little way off stood the remains of his great-grandfather's house, in remarkably good repair considering its long history.

There, too, was the huge oak, which Walt estimated to be nearly two hundred years old, and across the road was the large apple orchard; the trees planted years earlier by his Uncle Jesse were still thriving.

As they proceeded down the hill to the farm of Henry Jarvis and approached the house where, on May 31, 1819, Walt was born, he noticed the corn field in full tassel, the rye all cradled

103

neatly, and the oats being cut. Everything looked so fine, he said, that he began to have some doubts about the house. After inquiring of Mrs. Jarvis, whose father-in-law had bought this farm from Walt's father some sixty years earlier, all doubt was removed. This was indeed his birthplace.

After spending some time investigating the old Whitman burying ground on the hill, where Walt and his father had paused and pondered nearly thirty years before, they drove up the narrow winding road that led to the summit of Jayne's Hill, where Walt felt satisfied that it was as he remembered it—an exalted place from which one could look east for some thirty miles, northward to Long Island Sound, and toward the Great South Bay where a white haze on the horizon marked the shoreline of the Atlantic Ocean.

The next day, Whitman and Dr. Bucke were driven to the Van Velsor burial hill near Cold Spring, where Walt's maternal ancestors lay beneath the trees. A few of the graves had stones with faint epitaphs still visible. A light rain fell. As Walt breathed in the delicate odor of the moist woods, he thought back through sixty or more years to the days when his boisterous grandfather Cornelius and his sweet Quaker grandmother Amy in her white cap presided over the old farmhouse, where as a boy he had loved to visit. Now only a hole marked the cellar of the house and little piles of rubble were visible among the weeds. All else was gone. Even the lively little brook had dwindled to a mere trickle.

But nothing could erase the memory of that gay household, of the young colts in the pasture hobbling after their mothers, of grandfather Van Velsor's big market wagon standing there with its canvas canopy protecting the newly picked vegetables from the sun. Visits here had been among the happiest times of his childhood.

On their way back from Cold Spring, they stopped at the home of Warren Van Velsor, Walt's cousin. At first there was a slight pause, as Warren did not recognize this unusual looking stranger. Then he quickly stepped into the carriage with his visitors and drove away, leaving his family wondering what had happened. Upon returning home, he explained that he wished to extend his visit with Walt without delaying them, for it was approaching darkness. However, Whitman's reputation in his native area was still such that there was a reluctance among some to acknowledge a blood relationship to him.

One day in Huntington, Walt had dropped in at the office of the *Long Islander,* remarking on the many changes that time had wrought since the days when he bundled up his packet of papers and set forth to deliver them to his rural subscribers with his faithful horse Nina.

His visit to Huntington was recorded in a letter to the *New York Tribune* of August 7, 1881 written by Whitman himself, and of course in the *Long Islander,* which acknowledged his presence in a news item headed, "Walt Whitman in Town."

In a later issue, it printed the names of the men Whitman had met and reminisced with during the few days he spent in the area. In addition to the Van Velsors and Ben Doty of Cold Spring, there were Lemuel Carll, Jane Rome, and John Chichester, all of West Hills origin, Henry Lloyd, lawyer Charles R. Street, Albert Hopper, Smith Sammis, Thomas Rogers, John Fleet, and Charles E. Shepard, publisher of the *Long Islander.* Other Huntingtonians included Ezra Prime, who owned the local thimble factory, Henry Sammis, Thomas Atkins, owner of Huntington's leading drygoods establishment, a Mrs. Wood, and a Mr. Rusco.

No doubt many of these old friends and acquaintances were drawn more by curiosity than appreciation of his poetry, but Whitman was a man out of the ordinary and his fame could not be ignored, even in his own country town.

In his letter to the *Tribune,* Whitman had mentioned many of these friends by name and expressed his appreciation of their courtesies. The trip meant much to him. "Every day à point attained; every day something refreshing, Nature's medicine," he wrote. "The tree-lined roads and lanes, with their turns and gentle slopes, . . . after the main objects of my jaunt, made the most attraction as I rode around."

A few incidents that occurred during Walt's last visit to his native town did not come to light until much later. Whitman had urged one of his English friends to make the journey from Camden to Long Island and explore for himself the West Hills area about which he had spoken with such feeling. Along the road, this man encountered one Sanford Brown, who said he had known Whitman in his youth but had not seen him for some years, until one day a man came to his house and said, "Do you know anything about Walt Whitman?" Brown said he looked straight at the speaker and said, "Yes, and I know Walt Whitman." Then, holding out his hand, Walt said, "I see you do; but I have seen those that didn't," and then remarked on how many folks wanted to claim friendship with him now that he had become famous.

A man whose identity has been lost, who happened to drive Walt and Dr. Bucke to the depot as they were leaving town, recalled that as they arrived at the old Biggs house, Walt spied "Uncle" Sam Scudder, a boyhood friend who was boarding at the hotel. Whitman hobbled out of the wagon to meet Scudder. The two men embraced and kissed each other and as they parted, a good-sized greenback was slipped into Scudder's hand and plenty of tears filled the eyes of both men.

Whitman's last gift to his native Huntington was a copy of *Specimen Days and Collect,* an assortment of notes and jottings that had been accumulating through the years and was now published for the first time. Included in the collection were some pieces he had written during his last visit to Huntington and the story of his youthful venture as editor of the *Long Islander.*

Inscribed on the flyleaf of the book was the inscription:

Presented by the Author to the
Huntington Public Library
September, 1883

With a characteristic touch for keeping everyone informed of his doings, Whitman wrote to the *Long Islander* informing them of his gift to the library, which fact they were prompt to acknowledge.

His letter concluded, "I am about as usual in health &c. How I should like to pass another few days among the boys, (old and young) as I did two years ago there in Huntington, and perhaps it may come to pass again. Walt Whitman."[38]

But it never did come to pass. As long as he lived, Whitman treasured the memories of the final visit to his birthspot. It is certain that the friends he left behind would never forget it either.

20

Long Island Honors Its Poet

During his long illness, when Whitman was confined to his quarters in Camden, he quietly awaited his death, at peace with himself and the world. "The slower fainter ticking of the clock is in me . . . and soon the heart-thud stopping," he had written in one of his late poems entitled, "Good-Bye My Fancy!" He had calmly made preparations for his death, having planned for the disposition of his effects in a will and approved the design of the tomb that was to be his final resting place, with space provided for his parents and other members of his family.

On the evening of Saturday, March 23, 1892, as the light outside was failing and a gentle spring rain was falling, the end came. Whitman was buried in the vault at Harleigh Cemetery, where according to his wishes the bodies of his family were eventually placed.

Among the poems composed during Whitman's last years is the following:

Sail Out For Good, Eidolon Yacht!
Heave the anchor short!
Raise main-sail and jib—steer forth,
O little white-hulled sloop, now speed on really deep waters,
(I will not call it our concluding voyage,
But outset and sure entrance to the truest, best, maturest;)
Depart, depart from solid earth—no more returning to these
   shores,
Now on for aye our infinite free venture wending,
Spurning all yet tried ports, seas, hawsers, densities,
   gravitation,
Sail out for good, eidolon yacht of me!

The death of the poet was marked by hundreds of obituaries in papers all over the America he loved, many of which have been preserved in the Trent Collection at the Duke University library.

In addition to the *Eagle* and the *Times,* both of which honored their former editor by detailed biographies, Whitman's *Long Islander* devoted a front-page article of two columns to his life. It was introduced thus:

Walt Whitman Gone. The Good Gray Poet who died Saturday evening at his home at Camden, N.J., was a native of this town born in the village of West Hills on May 31, 1819. As the founder of the *Long Islander,* we owe a special tribute to the memory of this grand good old man who broke down his health in striving to alleviate the suffering of the sick and wounded soldiers of the army of the Potomac during the hottest part of the war. He was an occasional visitor to our village and his kindly thoughtful face will be remembered by many of us for the rest of our lives. We copy the following full account of Mr. Whitman's life from the New York *Tribune.* . . .

The April 2 issue of the Babylon *Signal* published a brief obituary notice, saying,

Walt Whitman, the famous poet died at his home in Camden, N.J. on Saturday in the 73rd year of his age. He was buried in Harleigh Cemetery near Camden. Mr. Whitman was born at West Hills near Huntington. When a young man he lived with his parents in a house then standing on what is now the farm of Charles C. Johnson at West Babylon. . . .

The *Republican Watchman* of Greenport on the same date, ventured beyond a mere epitaph, saying,

Walt Whitman, commonly called 'The Good Gray Poet,' after a long illness died at his home in Camden, New Jersey on March 26, aged 72 years, 9 months and 25 days, having been born at West Hills, town of Huntington, this county, on May 31, 1819. As in his life time there has been a widely variant opinion of his literary merit, so after his death the division in judgment as to his true place in the realm of letters will continue. He was one of the most distinguished men to whom Long Island ever gave birth.

For some peculiar or perverse reason, possibly because many residents of Greenport, where Walt's sister May Elizabeth still lived, would recall his perfect physique and superb state of health, the *Watchman* concluded, "An autopsy on the body revealed the fact that one lung was entirely gone and of the other only a little breathing spot was left, while the heart was surrounded by small abscesses and about 2½ quarts of water."

The life of Whitman was ended, but his life's work lives on in the never ending search by countless scholars to discover new shades of meaning in his poems, to penetrate the depths of his thinking. Not only are Whitman's concepts of the vast, unlimited oceans of space and the planets relevant to our times, when men in rockets orbit the moon, but his prophetic insights concerning the delicately balanced forces in our democracy, the ever present dangers as he saw them and wrote about them in *Democratic Vistas,* are as appropriate to the later decades of the twentieth century as they were in his time.

Whitman is honored now, in his own country and all over the world, wherever his works have been translated.

The museum at the Huntington Historical Society contains a very odd implement, a combination knife and fork, which according to a former Huntington resident was used by Walt Whitman in Camden for paring apples. In a letter to the Society, Harry C. Willetts recalls some interesting anecdotes of the days when as a boy he lived on Mickle Street near Walt's home and used to "toat Uncle Walt around in his road chair," for a two-cent piece, usually to the school yard where the children were at play.

The boys used to tease "Uncle Walt" about his whiskers and his long hair, Willetts said, "like all kids would do for fun."

One day he sat on the step with Whitman, and thoughtlessly

ran his foot over a colony of ants that were building their hills between the bricks on the pavement. Walt said to the boy, "O Sonny, I wouldn't do that. Look how long it takes those little ants to make their little homes." Willetts wrote that he never destroyed any ant hills from that moment on.

He mentioned Whitman's great fondness for apples, which the school children frequently brought him, along with the goodies that normally would have gone to their teachers.

The home-made knife and fork combination, which had been a gift to Whitman, had "on one end a hook like to clean our horses feet with," which Willetts said "used to tear his (Whitman's) pockets out and many a day I had to reach up his pant legs to find his knife and finally one day he got mad about it and gave it to me."

In Huntington, the large merchandise mart near the birthplace of the poet has been named for Whitman, as well as countless other smaller business enterprises. In West Babylon, a tablet on another emporium marks the spot where the Whitman family lived when Walt taught school there, near which was the pond where he thrashed the neighbor boy with his fish pole.

Several Long Island colleges and universities have dedicated halls or libraries to Whitman and have marked his birthday by special events through the years. Especially interested in the poet are the students who attend the large Walt Whitman High School at West Hills, less than a mile from the old Whitman family holdings.

After the Whitman family had sold their farm to Mr. Jarvis, the property passed through several hands. Eventually it was acquired by a real estate firm and subdivided into two-acre plots. The birthplace, which was advertised for sale in the columns of a New York paper, was purchased by a family named Watson, who managed to hold it until it could be made secure from the onslaughts of the bulldozer and land speculators.

Through many years of patient labor and sacrifice on the part of the little band of followers that comprised the Walt Whitman Birthplace Association, after options were given and then renewed, in order that further efforts to raise the necessary funds might be made, the birthplace was purchased. It was restored and furnished with appropriate pieces that had been solicited from the old families in Huntington.

However, it was soon realized that the expense of maintaining the house was considerable and staffing it with volunteer hostesses for any length of time was impractical.

During the term of Governor Averill Harriman, a bill was passed and signed by him, enabling New York State to accept and maintain Whitman's Birthplace, thus assuring its preservation and availability to the public.

From the days of the Jarvis ownership of the farm and throughout the occupancy of the Watson family, visitors had appeared from far and near, admirers of the poet, scholars, many of them distinguished writers themselves, wanting to see the Birthplace, and the bedroom where Whitman is said to have been born, approaching the threshold with subdued voices, and leaving with a feeling of having trod on hallowed ground.

There was a time when a few residents of West Hills challenged the assumption that this actually was the birthplace of Walt Whitman, being convinced themselves, from stories that had come down through their families, that the poet was actually born in the old family homestead. These persistent stories brought about an intense search of old records and deeds and a careful study of all of Whitman's notes and conversations in which he had referred to his birthplace.

Records of his last visit, in which he had referred to the Jarvis family who had bought the house and farm from his father, seemed to provide proof enough that this was in fact the place. Further corroboration, however, came in a letter from his younger sister Louisa Whitman Heyde, of Burlington, Vermont, in answer to an inquiry from Mrs. Romanah Sammis of Huntington, concerning the birthplace of her brother.

The letter said, in part, "My brother Walt Whitman was not born in the old Whitman homestead: he was born in the house you describe in your letter to me as the new house built in 1810 and owned by my father, as the birthplace of my brother Walt Whitman, born at West Hills, Huntington, Suffolk County, Long Island, N.Y. May 31, 1819. I would gladly send you a picture of his birthplace but think you have one. There are so many and you describe the house so plainly. . . ." The original of this letter is in the library of the Walt Whitman Birthplace Association.

Pilgrimages to the Birthplace have continued through the years, without abatement, sometimes solitary visitors, more on special occasions, such as the hundredth anniversary of Whitman's birth, when a large group of notables from the city came to honor him.

In 1955, the hundredth anniversary of the publication of Whitman's *Leaves of Grass,* his native town of Huntington marked the date with special displays at the Historical Society and the Huntington Public Library, programs at the schools, and feature articles in the *Long Islander.*

Since 1959 that newspaper has continued to celebrate the poet's birthday each May, devoting a page or more to various aspects of Whitman's life or works, edited each year by an outstanding Whitman scholar. These pages have become collectors' items.

However, the outstanding event to date occurred in May, 1969, Whitman's one hundred and fiftieth birthday, when the Town of Huntington issued a proclamation and many business, service, and cultural agencies as well as interested citizens joined in a coordinated effort to celebrate Walt Whitman, Huntington's most famous native son.

Featured were art and poetry contests, concerts, lectures by prominent Whitman scholars, displays of rare manuscripts and portraits, ending in a gala poetry reading by each of the noted Whitman scholars who had come from as far away as Texas and Ohio for this occasion.

The augmented anniversary page of the *Long Islander* included articles from leading scholars in France and Japan, and referred to Whitman's growing influence in the Soviet Union.

Visitors to the Birthplace come from all continents and from many countries of the world with perhaps the number of Japanese surpassing that of any other national group. Visitors trickle in from Alaska, Hawaii, and from each of the states on the continent. School children come in classes and individually and some day, perhaps, one of them will become a writer and follow in the path of Walt Whitman, the great poet of democracy.

Surely the name of Whitman will long be remembered and revered on his native Long Island.

Appendix

NOTES AND REFERENCES

1. *Year's Residence in America,* by William Cobbett. Sherwood, Neeley and Jones, London, 1818.
2. *Long Island Star.* October 2. 1845.
3. Huntington Town Records, Vol. I.
4. *Notes on Walt Whitman as Poet and Person,* by John Burroughs. American News Company, 1867.
5. "Two Old Family Interiors," from *Specimen Days,* by Walt Whitman.
6. *Faint Clews and Indirections,* by Walt Whitman, Trent Collection in the Duke University Library.
7. "The Maternal Homestead," from *Specimen Days,* by Walt Whitman.
8. *Faint Clews and Indirections,* by Walt Whitman. Trent Collection in the Duke University Library.
9. "Two Old Family Interiors," from *Specimen Days,* by Walt Whitman.
10. "Good-bye, My Fancy," by Walt Whitman. *Complete Prose Works,* Philadelphia, David McKay, 1892.
11. *Walt Whitman Looks at the Schools,* by Florence Bernstein Freedman. New York, Kings Crown Press, 1950.
12. *Uncollected Poetry and Prose of Walt Whitman,* edited by Emory Holloway. Vol. I, Introduction, XXVI, Note 9. Garden City, New York, Doubleday Page, 1921.
13. Biography of Elias Hicks by Walt Whitman, in *November Boughs.* Philadelphia, David McKay, 1888.
14. *Franklin Evans; or the Inebriate; A Tale of the Times,* a Novella, by Walt Whitman. New York, Random House, 1929.
15. *"The Shadow and Light of a Young Man's Soul,"* a story by Walt Whitman, *Uncollected Poetry and Prose of Walt*

115

Whitman, edited by Emory Holloway. Garden City, New York, Doubleday Page, 1921.

16. Walt Whitman's Early Life on Long Island, by Willis Steell. *Munsey's Magazine,* January, 1909.

17. Whitman's Teaching at Smithtown, 1837-1838, by Katherine Molinoff. No. 3 in a Series of Monographs on Unpublished Whitman Material. Brooklyn, 1942.

18. An Unpublished Whitman Manuscript: The Record Book of the Smithtown Debating Society, 1837-1838, by Katherine Molinoff. No. 1 in a Series of Monographs on Unpublished Whitman Material. Brooklyn, 1942.

19. *Tales of an Island and Its People,* by Clarence Ashton Wood. A booklet in the Files of the Walt Whitman Birthplace Association Library.

20. *Historic Huntington,* a booklet published by the Town on July 4, 1903, commemorating the 250th Anniversary of the Settlement of Huntington.

21. *Voices from the Press, A Collection of Essays, Sketches and Poems by Practical Printers.* New York, Charles B. Norton, 1850.

22. *Walt Whitman, Schoolmaster: Notes of a Conversation with Charles Roe,* by Horace Traubel. Walt Whitman Fellowship Papers No. 14; Philadelphia, April, 1895.

23. Charles E. Feinberg of Detroit, Michigan, a famous collector of Whitman Manuscripts.

24. *Personal Reminiscences of Men and Things on Long Island,* by Daniel Tredwell. Two Volumes of a Journal Published in 1912 by Charles A. Ditmas, Brooklyn.

25. From a letter in the Files of the Walt Whitman Birth-Place Association Library dated August 18, 1906, and written by Mrs. Lotta Rees. Mrs. Rees was a granddaughter of Warren Van Velsor, a member of Whitman's class in the Woodbury School.

26. *Visits to Walt Whitman in 1890-1891,* by J. Johnston and J. W. Wallace. London, Allen and Unwin, 1891.

27. "Starting Newspapers" from *Specimen Days,* by Walt Whitman.

28. From a newspaper clipping in the Trent Collection, Duke University Library.

29. "British Prison Ships," No. 5 of the Series of Brooklyniana Articles written by Walt Whitman. Vol. II *Uncollected Poetry and Prose* edited by Emory Holloway.

30. *Personal Reminiscences of Men and Things on Long Island,* by Daniel Tredwell. Two Volumes of a Journal Published in 1912 by Charles A. Ditmas of Brooklyn.

31. "A Whitman Collector Destroys a Whitman Myth." Charles E. Feinberg. Bibliographical Society of America, 1958.

32. "Old Poets," by Walt Whitman. *Complete Prose Works.* Philadelphia. McKay, 1892.

33. "Walt Whitman in Brooklyn," by W. E. Davenport. *Brooklyn Daily Eagle,* July 14, 1900.

34. From a Walt Whitman Manuscript owned by Edward Naumberg, Jr., and published in *Wake Magazine* in 1948.

35. A letter from Mrs. Edgar Reid of Tennent, N. J., to Bertha Funnell, dated January 20, 1964. Mrs. Reid is a niece of Anna Van Wyck.

36. "Walt Whitman's Early Life on Long Island," by Willis Steell. *Munsey's Magazine,* January, 1909.

37. One of the "Songs of the Open Road," by Walt Whitman.

38. *The Long Islander,* September 21, 1883.

ADDRESSES IDENTIFIED WITH WALT WHITMAN DURING HIS YEARS IN BROOKLYN:

1823 Front Street near Fulton Ferry—Residence.

1824 Cranberry Street opposite Plymouth Church—Residence.
Henry Street, north of Fulton Ave.—Residence.

1825 Johnson Street, north of Adams—Residence.
Johnson Street opposite last address—Residence.
Cranberry and Henry Streets, Apprentices Library—cornerstone ceremony where Whitman was kissed by Lafayette.

1826 251 Adams Street—Residence.

1827 41 Tillary Street—Residence.

1829 Adams and Concord Streets: School Whitman attended.

1831 149 Fulton Street: *Long Island Patriot* office where Whitman worked.

1832 Henry Street near Cranberry—Residence.
10 Liberty Street—Residence.

1833 120 Front Street—Residence.

1844 71 Prince Street—Residence.

1844 Skillman Street—Residence.

1846-1848 30 Fulton Street, office of the *Brooklyn Eagle* when Whitman was editor.

1846-1848 Boarded on Adams Street near Myrtle.

1848 110 Orange St. *Brooklyn Freeman* of which Whitman was first editor. Later it was published at 96 Myrtle Ave., at Fulton and Middagh, and at 335 Fulton, just south of Myrtle.

1849 106 Myrtle Ave.—Residence and Printing Shop.

1852 Cumberland St. north of Atlantic Ave.—Residence.

1854 142 Skillman St.—Residence. Wrote early poems of *Leaves of Grass* here.

1855 Ryerson St. north of Myrtle Ave.—Residence.
1856 91½ Classon Ave.—Residence.
1859 107 Portland Ave., north of Myrtle—Residence, where "When Lilacs Last in the Dooryard Bloom'd" was inspired. Lived here when brother George went to war with the 51st N.Y. Volunteers.

EDITORIALS WRITTEN BY WALT WHITMAN
Brooklyn Trees.

The beautiful large trees that stood so long on Dr. Hunt's old place, corner of Concord and Fulton streets, were cut down the other day, to gain a few inches more room to build brick and lime walls on. Now, though we hold to as little intermeddling as possible, by the press, with "private rights," we pity and denounce the taste of the Brooklyn Savings Bank* directors which achieved this work of death. Why didn't they let the trees stand and build a fine edifice a few feet further in?

We remember those beautiful trees from our childhood up. One of them was indeed a beauty—the great horse chestnut, with its magnificent bulge of verdure.

> Nor a prince,
> In all the proud old world, beyond the deep,
> E'er bore his crown as lofty as it
> Bore the green caronal where with
> God's hand had graced it.

But a few years ago there was also a splendid row of towering elms on the opposite side of Fulton Street, from James B. Clarke's old place up to Clinton street. One or two yet stand in front of the Rev. Mr. Jacobus' Church; but all the rest have been slaughtered.

It is perhaps expecting too much of those who newcome or newbuy in Brooklyn, that they should look upon such things with regard of love and sorrow. They never played under them in childhood. They don't remember them, identified with many a boyish spree and merry game. Into their hearts they have not rooted themselves "with hooks of steel," as their old roots have in the ground. But newcomers and speculators might at least have their eyes opened to the highest profits, for, even by the

*On September 7, 1870, Walt Whitman opened a savings account in the Brooklyn Savings Bank with $500.00. The account number was 101,398. *Walt Whitman Birthplace Bulletin,* January 1958.

sovereign rule, it is better to preserve the good looks of Brooklyn. And what great good looks there would be in Brooklyn, without its trees? Why every man who owns a lot should set out a tree or two in front of it for the dollars more it will make his lot bring.

We write this more for the future than the past. Because what is done cannot be undone. We have for a long time observed this practice of cutting down fine trees, to gain sometimes only twenty inches of room. In the name of both the past and the future, we protest against it.

Brooklyn Eagle, July 10, 1846

Editorials Selected from the Brooklyn Daily Times

Charles Dickens, some years ago, gave a picture of American Life and manners, in 'Martin Chuzzlewit,' which was not greatly relished by readers on this side of the Atlantic. They insisted that his portraitures of such people as Chollop, with their bowies and revolvers, were libelous, and that nothing answering to them could be found in nature, unless it were on the extreme limit of Western Civilization. But just look at the journals of the day, and say whether they were or were not. Mobs and murderers appear to rule the hour. Everybody who feels himself aggrieved, takes the law into his own hands and appeals to the revolver. The revolver rules, the revolver is triumphant. Juries discharge, without leaving their seats, the gallant and lion-hearted fellows who fire revolvers at unarmed men, and avenge their wrongs without the bore and expense of a criminal trial. Other equally gallant fellows, seeing them go unwhipped of justice, do not scruple at gratifying their little private animosities in a similar manner. No punishment follows crime. It is a moral impossibility to hang a bloody miscreant now-a-days, and it is altogether a beautiful, comfortable and safe state of Society that we are falling into. Reader, have you an enemy? Is he a chivalrous, gallant fellow? Go home and make your will.

November 7, 1857

Teachers—Shall Not They Too Be Taught?

Public Schools, and all other schools, are simply what the teachers of them are. Whatever characteristics and deficiencies are found in the teachers, the same return in the schools. For instance, we know a teacher who is dyspepsic, snappish, with no grace of manners, and no flowing sympathies; all these can be noticed, more or less, to re-appear in the school of which he is principal. He is learned in bookish facts—but in what makes a noble person he is almost altogether deficient.

Hardly a teacher now in any of the schools large or small, but needs discipline himself or herself. This is the great truth underlying the Normal Schools. Every teacher, male and female, should be required regularly to attend those schools all through their lives no matter how old they get to be. Does not the musician need unremitting practice? Does not the dancer, the painter, the orator? Just the same does every person engaged in teaching.

A grand Normal School in a city would be a fountain of life for the entire education of that city. It should be, in some respects, the noblest institution in the city. It should keep up with the age, not fall behind it in any respect. It should grade itself in Science etc. by the leading savants, the great reviews, the modern discoveries and announcements. It should be the rendezvous of all mental authority.

The physique also—the development of the body, muscle, strength, grace, agility, pure blood, sound organs—all these should be recognized and favored. The teachers themselves should be athletes.

We sometimes think when we look around that there are no good teachers at all in any of the schools. A person crammed with arithmetic, geography and grammar, we see him or her to be sure; but what a little way they go towards educing what can easily be educed out of a young human being.

July 10, 1857

The Weather

Yesterday was hot. Fat women felt fussy, and fanned furiously. Lean women leaned languidly on lounges or lolled lazily like lilies on a lake. Shabby, slipshod sisters sat silently and sadly sweating in the shade, while soiled and sozzling shirt-collars and sticky shirts stuck to such sapheads as stirred in the sun. Babies bawled lustily and bit bobbins and bodkins till bedtime. Literary gentlemen who undertook the heavy task of alliteration, became exhausted in the middle of a weather paragraph and gave it up for a cooler day.

August 13, 1857

124APPENDIX

BIBLIOGRAPHY

Books by and about Walt Whitman

1. *Complete Prose Works,* by Walt Whitman. Philadelphia, David McKay, 1892.

2. *Correspondence of Walt Whitman,* edited by Edwin H. Miller. 5 Volumes. New York, New York University, 1961-1969.

3. *Faint Clews and Indirections,* edited by Clarence Gohdes and Rollo Silver. Some Whitman Manuscripts. Durham, N.C. 1949.

4. *I Sit and Look Out,* edited by Emory Holloway and Vernolian Schwarz. A collection of editorials written by Whitman for the *Brooklyn Daily Times.* New York, 1932.

5. *In Re Walt Whitman,* edited by Horace Traubel, Thomas Harned, and Richard M. Bucke. Philadelphia, David McKay, 1893.

6. *New York Dissected: A Sheaf of Recently Discovered Newspaper Articles by the Author of Leaves of Grass,* edited by Emory Holloway and Ralph Adimari. New York, 1936.

7. *Notes and Fragments Left by Walt Whitman,* edited by Richard M. Bucke and A. Talbot. London, Ont., 1899.

8. *The Portable Whitman,* edited by Mark Van Doren. Selections from *Leaves of Grass, Specimen Days,* the 1855 Preface, *Democratic Vistas* and "A Backward Glance O'er Travel's Roads," New York, 1945.

9. *The Solitary Singer,* a critical biography of Walt Whitman by Gay Wilson Allen. New York University Press, 1967.

10. *The Uncollected Poetry and Prose of Walt Whitman,* edited by Emory Holloway. Two Volumes, Garden City, N.Y. Doubleday Page. 1921.

11. *Visits to Walt Whitman in 1890-1891,* by J. Johnston and J. W. Wallace. London, Allen and Unwin, 1891.

12. *Walt Whitman, an American,* a study in biography, by Henry Seidel Canby. Boston, Houghton Mifflin, Co. 1943.

13. *Walt Whitman,* by Gay Wilson Allen. Evergreen Profile Book 19. New York, Grove Press, 1961.

14. *Walt Whitman Looks at the Schools,* by Florence Bernstein Freedman. Columbia University, New York, 1950.

Pamphlets and Magazine Articles

1. A Series of Monographs on Unpublished Whitman Material by Katherine Molinoff.

Number One. "An Unpublished Whitman Manuscript; the Record Book of the Smithtown Debating Society, 1837-1838." Brooklyn, 1941.

Number Two. "Some Notes on Whitman's Family," Brooklyn, 1941.

Number Three. "Whitman's Teaching at Smithtown, 1837-1838." Brooklyn, 1942.

Number Four. "Walt Whitman and Southold." Brookville, N.Y. 1966.

2. Walt Whitman Fellowship Papers.

Number 10. "A Visit to West Hills," by Daniel G. Brinton. Philadelphia, 1894.

Number 14. "Walt Whitman, Schoolmaster: Notes of a Conversation with Charles A. Roe, 1894," by Horace L. Traubel. Philadelphia, 1895.

3. "The Good Gray Poet," by Richard Titherington, *Munsey's Magazine,* November, 1895.

4. "Walt Whitman's Early Life on Long Island," by Willis Steell. *Munsey's Magazine,* January 1909.

5. "Reminiscences of Walt Whitman," by John Townsend Trowbridge. *Atlantic Monthly,* January, 1902.

6. "The End of a Literary Mystery," by Frederick P. Hier, Jr. *American Mercury,* April, 1924.

7. "Walt Whitman," by Mrs. Rebekah Velsor Walters. *The Long Island Historical Society Quarterly, Vol. II No. I.* January, 1940.

8. "Walt Whitman at Smithtown," by Katherine Molinoff. *The Long Island Forum,* August, 1941.

9. "Walt Whitman and Long Island History," by Jesse Mer-

ritt. *The Long Island Historical Society Quarterly,* Vol. III No. 2, April, 1941.

10. Walt Whitman Centenary Edition of the *Bulletin* of the Brooklyn Institute of Arts and Sciences. May 3, 1919.

11. Special Walt Whitman Number of the American Book Collector, May, 1961.

12. "Walt Whitman, Poet of Democracy," by Cleveland Rodgers, Associate Editor of the *Brooklyn Eagle. The Mentor,* September, 1923.

Materials in Public and Private Libraries

1. *Brooklyn Daily Eagle:* Files in the library of the Long Island Historical Society in Brooklyn; files in the Brooklyn Public Library at Borough Hall.

2. *Long Islander:* Files in the library at the Huntington Historical Society at Huntington, N.Y.

3. *South Side Signal:* Files in the library at the Long Island Historical Society in Brooklyn.

4. *Republican Watchman:* Files in the library at the Suffolk County Historical Society at Riverhead, N.Y.

5. Miscellaneous manuscripts, letters, scrapbooks, and clippings in the Trent Collection at the Duke University Library, Durham, N.C.

6. Miscellaneous papers, pamphlets, scrapbooks, correspondence, and notes in the library of the Walt Whitman Birthplace Association, at the Whitman Birthplace, Huntington Station, N.Y.

Index

Alcott, Bronson, 84, 102
Allen, Gay Wilson, 35
American Eagle, 9
Amityville, 39
Aurora, The, 67

Babylon, 39, 40, 45, 46, 54, 63
Babylon Signal, 109
Beecher, Henry Ward, 76
Bennett, George C., 87
Bennett, James Gordon, 68
Block Island, 94
Boston, 89
Brenton, James J., 48, 50, 54, 55, 61
British, The, 15-18, 70
Brooklyn, Battle of, 15, 70
Brooklyn Daily Advertizer, 77
Brooklyn Daily Eagle, 68-71, 75, 77, 81, 87, 109
Brooklyn Freeman, 72, 73
Brooklyn Heights, 27, 29, 54
Brooklyn Navy Yard, 27, 70
Brooklyn Standard, 70
Brooklyn Times, 37, 73, 87-89, 109
Brooklyniana, articles, 70
Brown, Sanford, 63, 106
Brush, Hannah, 14
Brush, Major, 15
Bryant, William Cullen, 68, 76, 102
Bucke, R. M., 52, 103, 106
Burr, Aaron, 102
Burroughs, John, 13, 14

Camden, N. J., 6, 52, 53, 102, 106, 108-110
Chichesters of West Hills, 5, 15
Child And The Profligate, 6
Clark, Messrs., 33
Clements, Editor, 34, 51
Cobbett, William, 9-11
Cold Spring Harbor, 9, 16, 18, 19, 47, 63, 91, 104

Colyer Family, 78, 80
Commack, 8, 13, 45
Concord St. School, 27
Coney Island, 90
Cooper, James Fennimore, 92
Crescent, New Orleans, 71
Crowell, E. O., 50, 51

Darwin, Charles, 76
Davenport, W. E., 70
Democrat, The, 67
Democratic Review, 48, 67
Dix Hills, 63, 64, 67
Douglas, Frederick, 76

Eagle, *see Brooklyn Daily Eagle*
East Marion, *see* Marion
Emerson, Ralph Waldo, 5, 76, 82, 84, 102
Erie Canal, 8

Far Rockaway, 90, 91
Feinberg Collection, 60
Flushing, 55
Fort Greene, 88, 90
Free Inquirer, 29
Free Soil Party, 76
Freedman, Florence, 27, 28
Freeman, The, 72, 73
Fuller, Margaret, 91

Galow, Fred, 102
Gardiners Bay, 92, 95
Glen Cove, 92
Great South Bay, 36, 40, 90, 104
Greeley, Horace, 68
Greenport, 8, 64, 94, 95, 109, 110

Halleck, Benjamin B., 28
Harriman, Gov. Averill, 112
Hartshorne, William, 33
Hempstead, 35, 36, 60, 91

Hempstead Enquirer, 36, 48, 49, 50, 60, 61
Heyde, Hannah Whitman, 31, 112
Hicks, Elias, 11, 29, 30
Hicksville, 8, 78
Huntington, 7, 43, 47, 102, 104, 111-113
Huntington Historical Society, 73, 110, 113

Jackson, Andrew, 26, 102
Jamaica, 3, 8, 23, 25, 55, 65
Jayne's Hill, 7, 103, 104
Jefferson, Thomas, 33
Jericho, 9, 11, 22
Johnston, Dr. J., 6

Lafayette, General, 26, 102
Last Loyalist, 2
Leaves of Grass, 17, 40, 51, 81-84, 97, 102, 103, 113
Little Bayside, 56-58, 60, 65
Long Islander, The, 34, 43, 46-55, 60, 72, 93, 103, 105, 107, 109, 113
Long Island Daily Press, 55
Long Island Democrat, 50, 54, 55, 61, 62
Long Island Farmer, 55
Long Island Patriot, 33-35, 68, 81, 87
Long Island Star, 34, 35, 37, 68
Long Swamp, 40

Mann, Horace, 76, 87
Marion, 92, 94
Mirror, The, 35
Molinoff, Katherine, 41, 64
Monroe, President James, 8, 26
Montauk, 90, 93, 95, 98
Mount, William Sidney, 76
Mountain Mist Spring, 8
Murphy, Henry, 34, 68

New Orleans, 32, 71, 72
New Yorker, The, 73
New York Post, 68, 76, 77, 92
New York Sun, 73
New York Tribune, 68, 93, 105
Norwich, East, 35, 38
Notes And Fragments, 97

Oakley, Catherine Chichester, 73
Oakley, Zophar Brush, 73

O'Connor, William, 6
Old Salt Kossabone, 17
Orient, 8, 90, 92, 97
Oyster Bay, 38, 66
Oyster Pond, 8

Paine, Tom, 21, 29
Patriot, The see Long Island Patriot
Peace & Plenty Inn, 5, 15
Peconic Bay, 92, 93

Quaker, 11, 16, 29

Ray, Dr., 4-9
Republican Watchman, 109
Rockaway, 90, 91
Roe, Charles, 56-59
Rogers, Dr. David, 49
Rogers, Thomas, 105
Rome Brothers Print Shop, 81

St. Anne's Church, 27, 33
Salesman and Long Island Directory, 75, 93
Sammis, Daniel, 44
Sammis, Romanah, 112
Scudder's Hotel, 44
Scudder, Uncle Sam, 106
Shelter Island, 92, 95
Smith, "Bull Rider", 13,65
Smith, Col. Josiah, 15
Smithtown, 40-42, 45, 65
Songs of The Open Road, 85
Southold, 64, 66
Specimen Days, 12, 13, 40, 43, 52, 90
Specimen Days and Collect, 106
Spooner, Alden, 34, 68
Standard, The, 67
Star, see Long Island Star
Stuart, Carlos D., 73, 74
Suffolk Gazette, 34
Sun, New York, 73, 76
"Sun-Down Papers From The Desk Of A Schoolmaster", 56, 61, 62
Sutton, William H., 69

Tattler, The, 67
Thoreau, Henry David, 84, 102
Tomb Blossoms—A Story, 47
Traubel, Horace, 56, 59
Tredwell, Daniel, 60, 72, 73
Tribune, The see New York Tribune
Trimming, Square, 60, 91

Udall, General Richard, 39

Van Nostrand, Ansel, 64
Van Velsor Burying Ground, 104
Van Velsor, Amy, 16, 17
Van Velsor, Major Cornelius, 16, 17, 18, 21
Van Velsor Cousins, 18
Van Velsor, Warren, 104
Van Wyck, Anna, 79
Van Wyck, Ellen, 79
Van Wyck, Theodorus, 79
Voices of The Press, 48

Wallabout, 70
Wallace, J. W., 6
Walters, John, 80
Walters, Sarah Whitman, 78
Walt Whitman Birthplace Assoc., 111, 113
Walt Whitman Fellowship Papers, 56
Walt Whitman Looks At The Schools, 28
Washington, D.C., 100
Washington, George, 33
Washington Park, 88
Welsh, 16
West Babylon, 38, 111

West Hills, 7-9, 15, 17, 78, 103
Whitestone, 65
Whitman, Andrew, 32
Whitman, Edward, 32
Whitman, George, 82, 100-102
Whitman, Hannah Brush, 14
Whitman, Hannah Louise, 24, 68
Whitman, Jeff, 32, 68, 71, 90, 92
Whitman, Brother Jesse, 32, 68, 100
Whitman, Grandfather Jesse, 12, 14, 78
Whitman, Uncle Jesse, 78
Whitman, John, 12
Whitman, Joseph, 12, 13
Whitman, Louisa, 20-23, 31, 32, 79, 102
Whitman, Mary Elizabeth, 22, 39, 64, 110
Whitman, Nehemiah, 12-15
Whitman, Phoebe White, 13, 14
Whitman, Tredwell, 78
Whitman, Walter, 7, 12, 20-22, 31, 78-80
Whitney, Scudder, 63
Wild Frank's Return, 5
Willetts, Harry C., 110-111
Williams, 16
Wilmot Proviso, 71
Woodbury, 9, 16, 22, 63, 65, 78
Wright, Frances, 29